unclean

unclean

Meditations on

Purity, Hospitality,

and Mortality

Richard Beck

 CASCADE *Books* · Eugene, Oregon

UNCLEAN
Meditations on Purity, Hospitality, and Mortality

Copyright © 2011 Richard Beck. All rights reserved. Except for brief quotations in critical publications or reviews, no part of this book may be reproduced in any manner without prior written permission from the publisher. Write: Permissions, Wipf and Stock Publishers, 199 W. 8th Ave., Suite 3, Eugene, OR 97401.

Cascade Books
An Imprint of Wipf and Stock Publishers
199 W. 8th Ave., Suite 3
Eugene, OR 97401

www.wipfandstock.com

ISBN 13: 978-1-60899-242-3

Cataloging-in-Publication data:

Beck, Richard.

   Unclean : meditations on purity, hospitality, and mortality / Richard Beck.

   x + 202 p. ; 23 cm. — Includes bibliographical references.

   ISBN 13: 978-1-60899-242-3

   1. Hospitality—Religious aspects—Christianity. 2. Purity, Ritual—Biblical teaching. 3. Psychology, Religious. I. Author.

BL53 .B3631 2011

Manufactured in the U.S.A.

To Jana

There is love.

Go and learn what this means: "I desire mercy, not sacrifice."

—Matt 9:13

Do not call anything impure that God has made clean.

—Acts 10:15

. . . Love has pitched his mansion in
The place of excrement;
For nothing can be sole or whole
That has not been rent.

—W.B. Yeats

This is the meal pleasantly set . . . this is the meal
and drink for natural hunger,

It is for the wicked just the same as for the righteous . . .
I make appointments with all,

I will not have a single person slighted or left away,

The keptwoman and sponger and thief are hereby invited . . .
the heavy-lipped slave is invited . . . the venerealee is invited,

There shall be no difference between them and the rest.

—Walt Whitman

Contents

Acknowledgments

Expressions of Gratitude

to Charlie Collier and Wipf & Stock
for the invitation

to Halden Doerge
for the introduction to Arthur McGill

to Paul Rozin, Jonathan Haidt, Chen-Bo Zhong, Miroslav Volf,
Arthur McGill, Ben Witherington, Christine Pohl, Sheldon
Solomon, Jeff Greenberg, Tom Pyszczynski, Ernest Becker, Charles
Darwin, Martha Nussbaum, Charles Taylor, George Lakoff, Mark
Johnson, Walter Brueggemann, Mary Douglas, Peter Singer, Peter
Rollins, Jacques-Philippe Leyens, David Gilmore, Fernando Belo, S.
Mark Heim, Steven Pinker, Rene Girard, and William Miller
for the scholarship and ideas that made this book possible

to Andrea Haugen
for friendship, editing, and encouragement

to Kyle Dickson, Paul Morris, Mike Cope, Bill Rankin, Chris
Flanders, Kelly Young, Fred Aquino, David Dillman, Robert
McKelvain, Charles Mattis, Cole Bennett, Dan McGregor, Bill
Carroll, Adam Hester, Pat Brooks, Chris Heard, Angie McDonald,
Jonathan Wade, Jeff Reese, and Kenny Jones
for friendship and the life of the mind

to Paul Rozin and Alan Tjeltveit
for helpful feedback on my first paper relating disgust to theology

to Mark Love
for the ACU Lectureship forums (sorry about the controversy!),
friendship, and theological coaching

to the Sojourners adult bible class and Highland Church of Christ
for spiritual community and for tolerating my odd bible classes

to my parents—Richard and Paula Beck
for showing me the Way

to Brenden and Aidan
for joy

to Jana
for love

Introduction

Mercy and Sacrifice

Go and learn what this means: "I desire mercy, not sacrifice."

—**Matt 9:13**

1.

Imagine spitting into a Dixie cup. After doing so, how would you feel if you were asked to drink the contents of the cup?

Admittedly, this is a bizarre hypothetical and an odd way to start a book. For this, I apologize. But the Dixie cup hypothetical is really the best place to start, as it was the trigger, the key psychological insight, which culminated in the book you now have in your hands.

When I heard Paul Rozin, the world expert on the psychology of disgust and contamination, discuss his Dixie cup research I had been puzzling over the fragility of hospitality, the psychological obstacles to what Miroslav Volf calls "the will to embrace." Why do churches, ostensibly following a Messiah who broke bread with "tax collectors and sinners," so often retreat into practices of exclusion and the quarantine of gated communities? Why is it so difficult to create missional churches? In seeking answers to those questions I had been thinking a great deal about Jesus's response to the Pharisees in Matthew 9. In defending his ministry of table fellowship—eating with "tax collectors and sinners"—Jesus tells the Pharisees to go and learn what it means that God desires "mercy, not sacrifice."

Why, I wondered, are mercy and sacrifice antagonistic in Matthew 9? Why is there a tension between mercy and sacrifice? Of course, this tension might only be apparent and situational, two virtues that just happened to come into conflict in this particular circumstance. But the more I pondered the biblical witness and the behavior of churches, the more convinced I became that the tensions and conflict were not accidental or situational. I concluded that there was something intrinsic to the relationship between mercy and sacrifice that inexorably and reliably brought them into conflict. Mercy and sacrifice, I suspected, were mirror images, two impulses pulling in different directions.

Despite these suspicions, I was having difficulty penetrating the dynamics that linked mercy and sacrifice and fueled the tension between them. Perhaps surprisingly, the Dixie cup hypothetical helped lead me forward. I concluded that a particular psychological dynamic—disgust psychology—was regulating the interplay between mercy and sacrifice. How so? Consider the peculiarities of the Dixie cup test. Few of us feel disgust swallowing the saliva within our mouths. We do it all the time. But the second the saliva is expelled from the body it becomes something foreign and alien. It is no longer saliva—it is *spit*. Consequently, although there seems to be little *physical* difference between swallowing the saliva in your mouth versus spiting it out and quickly drinking it, there is a vast *psychological* difference between the two acts. And disgust regulates the experience, marking the difference. We don't mind swallowing what is on the "inside." But we are disgusted by swallowing something that is "outside," even if that something was on the "inside" only a second ago.

In short, disgust is a boundary psychology. Disgust marks objects as exterior and alien. The second the saliva leaves the body and crosses the boundary of selfhood it is foul, it is "exterior," it is Other. And this, I realized, is the same psychological dynamic at the heart of the conflict in Matthew 9. Specifically, how are we to draw the boundaries of exclusion and inclusion in the life of the church? Sacrifice—the purity impulse—marks off a zone of holiness, admitting the "clean" and expelling the "unclean." Mercy, by contrast, crosses those purity boundaries. Mercy blurs the distinction, bringing clean and unclean into contact. Thus the tension. One impulse—holiness and purity— erects boundaries, while the other impulse—mercy and hospitality—

crosses and ignores those boundaries. And it's very hard, and you don't have to be a rocket scientist to see this, to both erect a boundary and dismantle that boundary at the very same time. One has to choose. And as Jesus and the Pharisees make different choices in Matthew 9 there seems little by way of compromise. They stand on opposite sides of a psychological (clean versus unclean), social (inclusion versus exclusion), and theological (saints versus sinners) boundary.

In sum, the antagonism between mercy and sacrifice is *psychological* in nature. Our primitive understandings of both love and purity are regulated by psychological dynamics that are often incompatible. Take, for example, a popular recommendation from my childhood years. I was often told that I should "hate the sin, but love the sinner." Theologically, to my young mind (and, apparently, to the adults who shared it with me), this formulation seemed clear and straightforward. However, psychologically speaking, this recommendation was extraordinarily difficult, if not impossible, to put into practice. As any self-reflective person knows, empathy and moral outrage tend to function at cross-purposes. In fact, some religious communities resist empathy, as any softness toward or solidarity with "sinners" attenuates the moral fury the group can muster. Conversely, it is extraordinarily difficult to "love the sinner"—to respond to people tenderly, empathically, and mercifully—when you are full of moral anger over their behavior. Consider how many churches react to the homosexual community or to young women considering an abortion. How well do churches manage the balance between outrage and empathy in those cases? In short, theological or spiritual recommendations aimed at reconciling the competing demands of mercy and sacrifice might be psychological nonstarters. Spiritual formation efforts, while perfectly fine from a theological perspective, can flounder because the directives offered are psychologically naïve, incoherent, or impossible to put into practice.

In light of this situation, one goal of this book will be to examine the events in Matthew 9 from a psychological vantage point. The goal will not be to "psychoanalyze" the participants in the story but to understand the psychological tensions separating Jesus from the Pharisees, the same tensions we observe in churches who take different missional paths in the world. This will be the main plot of the story I have to tell. But there will be many surprising subplots as well.

2.

The central argument of this book is that the psychology of disgust and contamination regulates how many Christians reason with and experience notions of holiness, atonement, and sin. In a related way, the psychology of disgust and contamination also regulates social boundaries and notions of hospitality within the church. We will examine how this facet of disgust—distancing oneself from the "unclean"—is clearly on display in the events of Matthew 9. Finally, we will also explore how disgust and contamination psychology affect our experience of the body and soul, with a particular focus on how disgust is implicated in the scandal of the Incarnation. All in all, by the time we reach the final chapter of this book I expect many readers will be surprised at how much of the Christian experience is regulated or influenced by the psychological dynamics of disgust and contamination.

But before proceeding I would like, here at the beginning, to offer an apology for the approach used in this book. Let me start with a confession: I am not a theologian or biblical scholar. I am an experimental psychologist. Although I think I've done my homework, theologically and exegetically speaking, at the end of the day this book leans heavily upon the discipline of psychology. But I want to be clear that this book isn't solely or even primarily intended for social scientists. This book is for the church and for those leading the church in thought, word, and deed. It is my hope that theologians, biblical scholars, church leaders, spiritual directors, and pastoral counselors will find great value (and freshness) in the psychological approach pursued in this book. But I am a bit worried as there is always the danger that an interdisciplinary approach could fall between the cracks of academic and professional specialization. To prevent that from happening let me articulate, for any who find this necessary, how I think psychology can facilitate theological and moral reflection in both the academy and the church.

First, I want to be clear that I don't think theology can be reduced to psychology. Any appeal to psychology in this book is not an attempt to "explain" religious belief or behavior. The interplay between theology and psychology is interactive and dynamic. Theology—good or bad—affects how we experience the world, psychologically speaking. And psychological factors can affect and constrain theological reflection. For example, William James noted that rationality has a phenomenological feel (he called it the "sentiment of rationality"). We experience feelings of "rightness" and "wrongness" as we engage in intellectual inquiry, theological or not. More, James noted how certain hypotheses and intellectual options feel either "hot" or "cold" to us, either "alive" or "dead." In short, as we engage in theological reflection certain ideas woo and tempt us. Others leave us cold or repulsed. I've seen friends of mine, theologians and biblical scholars, wrinkle their nose, as if I forced them to smell rotten meat, when I've floated an idea they disagreed with. Theology, one finds, is a deeply emotional and visceral activity.

The point in all this is that there is an affective, experiential, and psychological aspect to theological reflection. We are pulled toward certain theological systems and repelled, even repulsed, by others. To be clear, I am not making a strong Humean claim that theology is simply a slave of the passions; rather, I am putting forth the Jamesian claim that reason can't be wholly detached from sentiment. Reason and emotion, the neuroscientists now tell us, are intimately linked. They cannot be dislocated. Consequently, it is important to attend to the psychological side of theological reflection, to ask why certain beliefs, systems or creeds seem "hot" or "cold" to us.

The danger of refusing to reflect upon the psychological dynamics of faith and belief is that what we feel to be self evidently true, for psychological reasons, might be, upon inspection, highly questionable, intellectually or morally. Too often, as we all know, the "feeling of rightness" trumps sober reflection and moral discernment. Further, we are often unwilling to listen to others until we are, to some degree, psychologically open to persuasion. The Parable of the Sower comes to mind.

This worry is less acute in the academy and seminary where critical thinking is prized and practiced. Not that professionals are immune to the passions: even the most intelligent and critical among us can fail to dispassionately consider arguments when a long-held and cherished position is at stake. No one likes to admit they are wrong, particularly if one's career or intellectual legacy is at stake.

But my deeper concern in this book is for the church, the people sitting in the pews. In the absence of advanced theological training or the daily immersion in critical give-and-take, the church will tend to drift toward theological positions that psychologically resonate, that "feel," intuitively speaking, true and right. Many of my theologian friends lament the quality of the theology they encounter in the church—in the pews, pulpits, prayers, songs, bulletin articles, and bible classes. They are appalled by the theological content of the top ten Christian bestsellers on Amazon. They are shocked, but they never ask the question the psychologist is trained to ask: what makes these theological beliefs so appealing? Why do they "feel right" to so many people? If we had good, solid answers to these questions we might be better positioned to educate and lead the church. This book attempts to provide one such analysis. It is an attempt to show how specific psychological dynamics make certain theological ideas more or less appealing. Unfortunately, as we will see, the psychological dynamics of disgust and contamination tend to pull us toward theological and moral dysfunction. To address this dysfunction we need to investigate the psychological pull, the magnetic attraction, of certain beliefs. The alternative is to simply throw up one's hands and lament, "How can people believe such rubbish?" when there are, in fact, answers to that question. Psychology, I think, can help uncover some of those answers.

I often use the following metaphor to explain to my students the relationship between psychology and theology. Consider the human sweet tooth. Humans, we know, crave fats and sugars. This is a universal feature of human psychology. Everybody loves fatty foods and sugar. Yet we know that a diet filled with sugar and fat is unhealthy, even dangerous. So we inhibit our sweet tooth. Moreover, we spend a great deal of effort investigating the optimal diet, the exact ratios of vitamins, vegetables, and dairy products. We even engage professionals, like signing up with WeightWatchers, to help us manage our sweet tooth.

But none of this eliminates the craving. The sweet tooth is always there, exerting a constant pull. And if we are not vigilant, that force tempts us back into an unhealthy diet.

Striving after good theology is similar to managing a sweet tooth. Psychological dynamics will always make certain theological systems more or less appealing. And yet psychologically appealing and intuitive theological systems are not always healthy. In short, these psychological dynamics function as a sweet tooth, a kind of cognitive temptation that pulls the intellectually lazy or unreflective (because we are busy folk with day jobs) into theological orbits that hamper the mission of the church. As with managing the sweet tooth, vigilance and care are needed to keep us on a healthy path.

This book is about a particular kind of sweet tooth. It is an analysis of how a certain psychological system, the system that regulates the emotion of disgust and the attributions of contamination, captures notions of holiness, morality, sin, salvation, and much, much more. And like the sweet tooth, when aspects of Christian life are "captured" and regulated by disgust psychology a variety of unhealthy outcomes emerge—from the Macbeth Effect, to scapegoating, to practices of exclusion, to a Gnostic flight from the body. This book walks through these unhealthy outcomes, showing how each is the product of a theological sweet tooth, one that cannot be escaped or eliminated, only monitored and resisted.

3.

Before we get started, an overview of the book.

To understand the unhealthy and pernicious consequences of disgust and contamination psychology in the life of the church we need to review the empirical literature concerning both disgust and contamination. Part 1—*Unclean*—is a primer on the psychology of disgust and contamination. It is a fascinating body of literature. Disgust is a surprising emotion. Beyond the emotion of disgust, Part 1 will also survey the literature concerning contamination. The two are intimately related as disgust is often triggered by an appraisal of contamination. If a hair in your soup triggers a judgment of contamination then the prospect of eating the soup is disgusting. The theological relevance of contamination psychology is that contamination appraisals are governed by a peculiar logic that is often characterized by what psychologists call "magical thinking." For example, the notion of contact is critical to judgments of contamination. Did the hair come into contact with my soup? In a similar way, the Pharisees were offended by the *contact* between Jesus and sinners in Matthew 9. To external observers it might seem strange that physical proximity or physical touch could "defile" a person. But contamination appraisals are governed by these seemingly illogical notions. The problem for the church comes when this "magical thinking" is allowed to affect how we think about hospitality or morality in the life of the church.

After the primer of disgust and contamination psychology in Part 1 we begin to survey the effects of disgust, theologically and ecclesially, across three different domains. Part 2—*Purity*—discusses how disgust psychology regulates aspects of the moral domain. As William Miller observes in his book *The Anatomy of Disgust*, "moral judgment seems almost to demand the idiom of disgust."[1] Within Christianity we'll examine how sin comes to be understood as pollution or defilement, the state of being "unclean." Given this view of sin, salvation, particularly soteriological metaphors based upon the Day of Atonement in the Hebrew Scriptures, is understood to be a washing, purification, or cleansing.

Beyond this general metaphor for sin and salvation, we will also examine how particular sin domains are uniquely regulated by purity metaphors (e.g., sexual "purity"). None of this would be particularly worrisome if it were not for the fact that disgust and contamination psychology structures the way these metaphors are used and experienced. Very often, due to the way psychology regulates purity categories, these metaphors can have noxious consequences. For example, as we will see, one feature of contamination psychology is the attribution of *permanence*. Once an object is deemed to be contaminated there is very little that can be done to rehabilitate the object. Consequently, sin categories that are psychologically structured by purity metaphors are experienced as "permanent" and are difficult if not impossible to rehabilitate. For sins of this nature, once purity is "lost" there is no going back. At least that is how we *experience* purity violations. Pastorally speaking, this may be why sexual sins, which are often uniquely structured by the purity metaphor in many churches, elicit more shame and guilt. In short, although a church might claim that all sins are "equal" (in their offensiveness to God), sins have different psychological experiences. This is largely due to the fact that

1. Miller, *Anatomy of Disgust*, xi.

sin categories are regulated by different metaphors, each activating different psychological processes. Sins might indeed be equal, theologically speaking, but the *experience* of a given sin can be very, very different depending upon the psychology regulating the experience.

Part 3—*Hospitality*—examines the social functions of disgust. Disgust properties are frequently imputed to despised groups. As William Miller has observed, "Disgust and misanthropy seem to have an almost inevitable association."[2] We find people "disgusting" or "revolting." Social disgust is clearly on display in Matthew 9. We also see it in Peter's vision of "unclean" animals in Acts 10. The voice from heaven tells Peter that his objection to eating unclean animals is in error: "Do not call anything unclean that the Lord has made clean." The vision is ostensibly about the Jewish *purity* codes regarding foodstuffs. But the heart of the vision is *sociological*, the critique that the Jewish leaders of the church were not taking the gospel to the Gentiles. In short, disgust properties create sociological barriers and motivate acts of exclusion. In mild forms this exclusion is simple avoidance or contempt. In extreme forms the act of exclusion is genocidal.

Part 4—*Mortality*—examines the existential aspects of disgust. There are many disgust stimuli that have little to do with food, morality, or social exclusion. For example, corpses, gore, deformity, and bodily fluids are reliable disgust triggers. Researchers have noted that these stimuli share a common core: each functions as a mortality reminder. We are existentially unsettled by the fact that we have a physical body that bleeds, oozes, and defecates. We are shocked to find that we are vulnerable to injury, illness, and death. Historically speaking, the physical body has always been a source of scandal within the Christian tradition. The physical body is illicit, craven, pornographic. Such body-related disgust is found to serve an existential function: it enables us to repress our fears of death.

The fact that disgust helps to fend off or repress fears about death and our physical dependencies wouldn't be so worrisome if it were not for the fact that a denial of our need, vulnerability, and dependency hardens our hearts when we see need exhibited in others. We don't want to be reminded of such things. As Arthur C. McGill observes in his book *Death and Life: An American Theology*,

2. Ibid., xiv.

Americans "devote themselves to expunging from their lives every appearance, every intimation of death . . . . All traces of weakness, debility, ugliness, and helplessness must be kept away from every part of a person's life."[3] We pretend, continues McGill, that "the lives we live are not essentially and intrinsically mortal."[4] Consequently, to protect this illusion—that death and decay are not at work in our lives—we hide our eyes from the old, sick, deformed, ugly, and needy. As McGill notes, we create institutions and structures that "compel all such people to be sequestered where we cannot see them."[5] The emotion of disgust prompts most of this activity, acting as an existential buffer. Disgust motivates us to avoid and push away reminders of vulnerability and death, in both others and ourselves. What is needed to combat this illusion is a church willing to embrace need, decay, and vulnerability. Such a church will share similarities with the liberal society Martha Nussbaum envisions in her book *Hiding from Humanity*:

> A society that acknowledges its own humanity, and neither hides us from it nor it from us; a society of citizens who admit that they are needy and vulnerable, and who discard the grandiose demands for omnipotence and completeness that have been at the heart of so much human misery, both public and private.[6]

In chapter after chapter we will encounter a common theme: although disgust has some positive aspects, its role and influence in the life of the church is deeply problematic. I've already highlighted a few of these problems. Given these problems we are led to ask, what are we to do with disgust in the life of the church? How are we, returning to Matthew 9, to keep sacrifice from trumping mercy? The final chapter of the book attempts, in a preliminary way, to answer these questions.

3. McGill, *Death and Life*, 26.

4. Ibid., 27.

5. Ibid., 19.

6. Nussbaum, *Hiding from Humanity*, 17.

PART 1

Unclean

Humans are most likely the only species that
experiences disgust, and we seem to be the only
one capable of loathing its own species.

—William Miller, *The Anatomy of Disgust*

1

Darwin and Disgust

The term "disgust" in its simplest sense, means something offensive to the taste. It is curious how readily this feeling is excited by anything unusual in the appearance, odour, or nature of our food. In Tierra del Fuego a native touched with is finger some cold preserved meat which I was eating at our bivouac, and plainly showed utter disgust at its softness; whilst I felt utter disgust at my food being touched by a naked savage, though his hands did not appear dirty. A smear of soup on a man's beard looks disgusting, though there is of course nothing disgusting in the soup itself. I presume that this follows from the strong association in our minds between the sight of food, however circumstanced, and the idea of eating it.

—**Charles Darwin**, *Expression of the Emotions in Man and Animals*

1.

Disgust is a surprising emotion. It is startling how many aspects of daily existence are affected by this emotion. In the morning I rise, brush my teeth, shower, and apply deodorant. I don't want to smell bad to others. I don clean clothing and will worry later if my fly is down during my lectures. I eat with my mouth closed. I avoid creepy people in public places. I wrinkle my nose at the food left too long in the fridge. I spray air freshener in the workplace bathroom after I'm done. I feel revulsion at the crime I hear about on TV. I am repulsed by how much blood was in the R-rated movie. I tell my son to apologize for farting or burping at the dinner table. I worry about shaking hands after my coworker sneezed into his own. I kiss my wife on the mouth but am revolted at the prospect of greeting others this way. I watch a person get baptized with water at my church. I sing songs about being "washed in the blood of the Lamb." I struggle with my not-so-clean conscience. I chase the bug my wife saw in the bathroom. I send my soup back because I found a hair in it. I read about a genocide, an act of ethnic cleansing.

From dawn to dusk, disgust regulates much of our lives: biologically, socially, morally, and religiously.

The varieties of disgust are built atop a common psychological foundation. Consequently, to understand how disgust affects us, how it can regulate aspects of our social or moral lives, it will be necessary to understand the basic psychology of the disgust response. Having a firm grasp of the psychological fundamentals of disgust will be important, and illuminating, as we go forward.

Charles Darwin is often credited with initiating the modern study of disgust in his book *Expressions of the Emotions in Man and Animals*. *Expressions* is now recognized as a seminal work in the field of evolutionary psychology. In *Expressions* Darwin documented facial, physiological, and behavioral similarities between humans and animals when we experience basic emotional states. For example, both dogs and humans expose their teeth when angry. Chimps and humans both grin when anxious. Our hair stands on end, like cats, when we are scared.

Darwin devotes a chapter in *Expressions* to the emotion of disgust. As seen in the quote at the start of this chapter Darwin links disgust with food and the prospect of eating something that has come into contact with a polluting influence, like the touch of a "naked savage."[1] Darwin also notes that disgust is characterized by a distinctive facial response seen in the wrinkling of the nose and the raising of the upper lip. Due to the work of the psychologist Paul Ekman we know that this distinctive facial expression is a cultural universal.[2] All humans

1. Darwin, *Expressions*, 256.
2. Ekman and Friesen, "Constants across Cultures," 124–29.

make the same face when experiencing disgust. Disgust, it appears, is an innate feature of a shared and universal human psychology.

The distinctive movements of the mouth, eyes, and nose involved in the facial expression of disgust are due to a constriction in the levator labii muscle region of the face.[3] This constriction is characteristic of an oral/nasal response to reject something offensive that has been eaten. Linked to this response is the impulse to spit. As Darwin notes, "spitting obviously represents the rejection of anything offensive from the mouth."[4] Finally, if swallowed, the experience of nausea promotes vomiting, forcefully expelling the offensive object from the body.

At its root, then, disgust is found to be involved in monitoring oral incorporation (mainly eating) and keeping track of food aversions. The psychologist Paul Rozin calls this *core disgust*.[5] Basically, core disgust monitors what we put in our mouth. Core disgust is an innate adaptive response that rejects and expels offensive or toxic food from either being eaten or swallowed.

We have only just begun our survey of disgust psychology and already two important observations have been made. First, disgust is a *boundary* psychology. Disgust monitors the borders of the body, particularly the openings of the body, with the aim of preventing something dangerous from entering. This is why, as seen in Matthew 9, disgust (the psychology beneath notions of purity and defilement) often regulates how we think about social borders and barriers. Disgust is ideally suited, from a psychological stance, to mark and monitor interpersonal boundaries. Similar to core disgust, social disgust is triggered when the "unclean," sociologically speaking, crosses a boundary and comes into contact with a group identified as "clean." Further, as we will see in Part 2 of this book, the boundary-monitoring function of disgust is also ideally suited to guard the border between the holy and the profane. Following the grooves of core disgust, we experience feelings of revulsion and degradation when the profane crosses a boundary and comes into contact with the holy.

3. Chapman et al., "In Bad Taste," 1222–26.
4. Darwin, *Expressions*, 261.
5. Rozin et al., "Disgust," 637–53.

Beyond functioning as a boundary psychology we have also noted that disgust is an *expulsive* psychology. Not only does disgust create and monitor boundaries, disgust also motivates physical and behavioral responses aimed at pushing away, avoiding, or forcefully expelling an offensive object. We avoid the object. Shove the object away. Spit it out. Vomit.

This expulsive aspect of disgust is also worrisome. Whenever disgust regulates our experience of holiness or purity we will find this expulsive element. The clearest biblical example of this is the scapegoating ritual in the Hebrew observance of the Day of Atonement (cf. Leviticus 16), where a goat carrying the sins of the tribe is expelled into the desert. The scapegoat is, to use the language of disgust, spit or vomited out, forcefully expelling the sins of the people. In this, the Day of Atonement, as a purification ritual, precisely follows the logic of disgust. The scapegoating ritual "makes sense" as it is built atop an innate and shared psychology. The expulsive aspect of the ritual would be nonsensical, to either ancient or modern cultures, if disgust were not regulating how we reason about purity and "cleansing."

The worry, obviously, comes when people are the objects of expulsion, when social groups (religious or political) seek "purity" by purging themselves through social scapegoating. This dynamic—purity via expulsion—goes to the heart of the problem in Matthew 9. The Pharisees attain their purity through an expulsive mechanism: expelling "tax collectors and sinners" from the life of Israel. Jesus rejects this form of "holiness." Jesus, citing mercy as his rule, refuses to "sacrifice" these people to become clean.

2.

One of the interesting facets of disgust is that it isn't an emotion we have at birth. Small children are notorious for having little to no disgust response. Babies will put just about anything in their mouths. I remember when my son picked some gum off the floor in a subway station in New York City and starting eating it. (I have some levator labii muscle constriction going on right now recalling the incident.)

This curiosity about disgust is combined with another: we eat only a small fraction of the edible foodstuffs in our ecosystem. There are lots of things we could eat but just don't. Americans, for instance, don't eat bugs, worms, dogs, animal brains, and so on. We find these very legitimate foodstuffs to be, well, disgusting. This phenomenon is observed the world over. Although tastes vary widely from culture to culture, all cultures have foods that elicit disgust that, from a purely dietary stance, are edible and even nutritious.

What can explain these peculiarities? Why does disgust emerge late in development and why do we feel disgust toward foods that are potentially nutritious? The answer has to do with the fact that humans can live in just about every terrestrial ecosystem. The food available across these ecosystems varies considerably. Consequently, it would be maladaptive for humans to have innate and very particular food preferences. Given the range of habitats humans can find themselves in, a degree of flexibility is warranted to sync tastes with available foodstuffs. So when a child is born she doesn't have any innate food preferences. She will, as we said, eat just about anything. In short, children are naturally open to the foodstuffs around them no matter where they are born. The delayed onset of disgust allows us to acquire food preferences across a diversity of ecosystems, fitting taste to environment and culture.[6]

But a willingness to eat just about anything in a given ecosystem can also be dangerous. Within any ecosystem there will be objects and foodstuffs that are toxic, disease vectors, or simply not nourishing. Consequently, the early disgust-free window of infancy and early childhood eventually evaporates. Sooner or later, disgust emerges, effectively locking in our food preferences. The onset of disgust protects us from being too adventurous in our dietary habits. It appears, then, that disgust develops in a way similar to language. As with an openness to all foodstuffs, a child is born with the facility to learn any human language. Eventually, after a period of time (called a sensitive period) this natural facility to acquire language is lost and the Mother Tongue is "locked in." After the sensitive period passes a new language can be learned, as new food preferences can also be acquired, but this has to be done in a more effortful and deliberative manner (e.g., language school or the intentional sampling of foreign cuisine).

6. Fallon et al., "Child's Conception," 566–75.

What is the relevance of all this for our purposes? Disgust, as we have just seen, has a degree of plasticity; it is molded to fit a given culture. We don't see this feature in other emotions. The core triggers for happiness, fear, sadness, or anger appear to be fairly stable and consistent across cultures. But disgust stimuli can be highly variable from culture to culture. This seems to be due to the fact that disgust, unlike other emotions, has a sensitive period. During this sensitive period, when disgust is unattached to particular stimuli, disgust can be captured and harnessed by a culture, connecting disgust to stimuli unrelated to food or food aversions. This is the reason why we find disgust—a food aversion system—associated with social, moral, and religious domains. Due to the sensitive period disgust is a promiscuous emotion, attaching to a wide variety of stimuli, many unrelated to food.

How promiscuous is disgust? Paul Rozin and colleagues have observed that the following stimuli tend to be reliable disgust electors, at least among North Americans:

1. Food
2. Body products (e.g., feces, vomit)
3. Animals (e.g., insects, rats)
4. Sexual behaviors (e.g., incest, homosexuality)
5. Contact with the dead or corpses
6. Violations of the exterior envelope of the body (e.g., gore, deformity)
7. Poor hygiene
8. Interpersonal contamination (e.g., contact with unsavory persons)
9. Moral offenses[7]

Some of this list is reasonable if disgust is primarily a response protecting us from eating things that might be toxic or a disease vector. However, much of this list has little to do with eating or oral incorporation. For example, as we've noted, disgust often regulates moral, social, and religious experiences.

Psychologists have attempted to look for patterns among these disgust domains. Not surprisingly, the classification scheme proposed

7. Haidt et al., "Individual Differences," 701–13.

by Paul Rozin has been influential.[8] Specifically, Rozin breaks the disgust domains down this way:

1. *Core Disgust (food)*: Revulsion centered on eating and oral incorporation: the adaptive core of disgust.
2. *Sociomoral Disgust (moral offenses, social groups)*: Revulsion centered on moral and social judgments: the aspect of disgust related to issues of hospitality in Matthew 9.
3. *Animal-Reminder Disgust (gore, deformity, animals, hygiene, death)*: Revulsion centered on stimuli that function as death/mortality reminders: the existential aspect of disgust.

In Parts 2 through 4 of the book we'll work through each of these domains. We'll start with how disgust is related to morality, move on to the social facets of disgust, and conclude with the existential aspects of disgust. Before concluding this chapter, however, I'd like to point out a connection that I will return to at the end of this book. I want to make this observation here, at the beginning, so that you can ponder the implications in the chapters to come.

Specifically, consider the disgust domains in relation to the Eucharist. I find it intriguing and suggestive that the three disgust domains map onto, almost perfectly, the dominant images and metaphors of the Lord's Supper:

1. *Core Disgust*: Food—oral incorporation—is at the center of both the psychology of disgust and the Eucharist.
2. *Sociomoral*: Socially, the Eucharist echoes and reenacts Jesus's ministry of table fellowship. Coming to the Lord's Table we are to "welcome each other, as Christ has welcomed us." Morally, the Eucharist echoes the Day of Atonement, the ritual where the sins of Israel were "cleansed." In a similar way, Christians remember that the blood of Jesus "continually cleanses us."
3. *Animal-Reminder*: The Eucharist has strong, even scandalous, cannibalistic overtones. The emblems—bread and wine—represent the body and blood of Jesus. Consequently, the gritty, Incarnational and embodied aspects of the life of Jesus (and the church) are graphically confronted in the Lord's Supper.

8. Rozin et al., "Disgust," 637–53.

Food, hospitality, salvation, the physical body: every facet of disgust is implicated and blended in the Eucharist. We eat. We welcome. We are purified. We confront the scandal of the Incarnation. Why this particular combination of images? And is it simply a coincidence that the Eucharist conflates the disgust domains into the ritual?

I will return to these questions in the final chapter. I make these observations now so that they can be pondered in the pages that follow. Suffice it to say, I think the Eucharist, providentially so, is engaged in shaping and reshaping how we think about purity, hospitality, and mortality: the three domains, as we have seen, deeply affected by disgust psychology.

2

Contamination and Contagion

A particularly important feature of contagion, paralleled by disgust, is the journey from the physical to the moral. Although moral contagion is often indelible, it is sometimes treated as if it is physical.

—Paul Rozin, Jonathan Haidt, and Clark McCauley

1.

In his book *Expression of Emotions in Man and Animals*, Darwin equated disgust with *distaste*. This is reasonable; the Latin origins of the word *disgust* mean "to taste bad."

But disgust is more than simple distaste. Many things taste bad but are not disgusting, like coffee or lemons. Generally speaking, disgust involves the feeling of *revulsion*, a visceral, almost nauseous, response. And this revulsion is very often triggered by a judgment or appraisal of contamination or pollution. A foodstuff might be perfectly edible and attractive but if it comes into contact with a polluting influence (e.g., the proverbial fly in one's soup) the food is "ruined" and the prospect of eating it becomes disgusting.

In short, beyond monitoring the boundary of the body and rejecting objectionable objects from the body, disgust also monitors

the environment, marking sources of contamination and pollution.[1]
Many of these stimuli are legitimate vectors for disease (e.g., feces)
while others are the product of our learning histories (e.g., food aversions due to food poisoning). However, many sources of contamination are driven by culture and have little or nothing to do with
food. A behavior might be experienced as a pollutant to a person's
soul, soiling our conscience. A person's presence in the church might
be experienced as offensive or inappropriate. In short, as we noted
in the last chapter, although contamination monitoring is at root
healthy and adaptive, we should worry when judgments of contamination are extended into the religious, moral, and social domains.
Given that contamination appraisals are built atop a more primitive
food-aversion system we should worry about certain psychological
dynamics (e.g., revulsion), perfectly legitimate in the domain of
food choice, being imported into the life of the church. Disgust and
contamination are powerfully aversive experiences and we should be
wary when these experiences are directed toward others or the self.
However, to effectively monitor and thwart contamination appraisals
it will be important for us to come to grips with the unique "logic" of
contagion and pollution. How does defilement work?

2.

Imagine I offer you a glass of juice. But before I hand the glass over
to you I drop a cockroach in the juice, stir it around, and then remove the bug from the glass. Will you drink the juice? Most people
don't. There is nothing surprising in this reaction. It's a simple case
of contamination psychology at work. The bug—the contaminating
object—has come into contact with the foodstuff and this ruins the
juice. After contact with the bug the juice is judged as impure, unclean, polluted, and contaminated.

But here is where things start to get interesting. In his laboratory, Paul Rozin has gone on to ask some additional questions regarding the ruined glass of juice. Of course you won't drink the juice
after a bug has been swirled around in it, but what if we filtered the

---

1. Rozin et al., "Disgust," 637–53.

juice through one of those filters that are used to purify tap water? Would you drink the juice after this filtering? What if we filtered the juice, boiled it, and filtered it again? Would you drink the juice then? Interestingly, most people still refuse to drink the juice despite knowing, rationally speaking, that the boiled and filtered juice is purer than most tap water. Intellectually, people understand that the boiled and filtered juice is clean. The juice has been sanitized before their very eyes. And yet people still reject the juice. Even while they admit the illogical nature of their response.

What Rozin's research helps us see, vividly so, is that judgments of contamination play by their own rules. And these rules are very often contrary and impervious to logic and reason. Rationally, I judge the juice as sanitized. At the same time a contamination-based appraisal is also at work. This appraisal continues to judge the juice as unfit to drink. Reason and contamination psychology have come into conflict.

This facet of disgust psychology, that it plays by its own rules, will prove important in the chapters to come. For example, when understandings of purity, sin, salvation, and holiness are regulated or influenced by disgust psychology we unwittingly import a contamination-based reasoning into the life of the church. And, as we have just seen, contamination-based reasoning, being governed by a unique set of rules, is often immune to reason and rationality.

3.

What are the rules governing judgments of contamination? How does the logic of contamination work? (And to be clear, the phrase "contamination logic" is using the word "logic" to speak about the internal mechanics and rules that govern contamination judgments. The logic here is internal to the system, the functioning of its inner workings. From the outside, as mentioned above, contamination appraisals can be quite illogical when assessed by the standards of formal reasoning and rationality. Externally, judgments of contamination are oftentimes bizarre and irrational.)

Broadly speaking, judgments of contamination demonstrate a logic very similar to the logic one observes in what is known as sympathetic magic.[2] Sympathetic magic is an anthropological term that has been used to characterize a variety of primitive beliefs about how spiritual or magical artifacts and rituals might have effects upon other objects. Take, as an example, the magical idea of *similarity* seen in the voodoo doll. According to the logic of sympathetic magic, similarity creates a "connection" between two objects. Thus the voodoo doll is made to look like the person I want to curse. The similarity between the doll and target is judged to be important for the creation of a causal link.

It was once assumed that sympathetic magic only characterized the religion and spirituality of primitive peoples. Modern scientific people were believed to be immune to the fanciful reasoning observed in primitive magic. Logically we moderns know that, just because a doll looks like a person, there is no reason to assume a causal connection between the two. But as recent psychological research has repeatedly shown, modern scientifically literate people often make judgments of just this sort. And, as we will also see in later chapters, this "magical thinking" is very often carried over into the life of the church.

To illustrate magical thinking at work in modern people consider some other examples from Paul Rozin's laboratory. Rozin has offered people brownies baked to look like doggie poop. Or asked people to drink lemonade from a never-been-used and sterilized bedpan. And time after time, people refuse to eat or drink. Rationally, the participants know that what looks like dog poop is actually a brownie. Rationally, they know that the yellow liquid is lemonade, not urine. But the brownie *looks like* dog poop and the lemonade *looks like* urine. And that's enough to trigger disgust. Even though we know that this response is irrational.

In short, something like the magical law of similarity appears to be operative. If two things look similar our mind has trouble separating them. Even if, logically, we know the truth of the matter. Magical thinking tends to override reason.

Take, as another example, the magical notion of *contact*. The voodoo doll must involve more than similarity. Somehow the doll and the target must make contact. This is often accomplished by taking something from the target (e.g., hair) and incorporating it into the

---

2. Nemeroff and Rozin, "Makings of the Magical Mind," 1–34.

doll. This contact creates a connection that the voodoo practitioner hopes to exploit.

Like with the law of similarity, we see this law of contact also at work in disgust and contamination responses. Consider again the cockroach and the juice. Why will we not drink the juice after it has been sanitized? Our feelings seem to be governed by the magical law of contact. That is, once a connection is made between the cockroach and the juice they forever remain in contact. The rule seems to be "once in contact, always in contact."

Now a theologian might be wondering at this point: what do cockroaches in juice or poop-shaped brownies have to do with the life of the church? That's a good question. The answer is that the magical thinking found in contamination judgments is regularly imported into the moral, social, and religious domains. To illustrate this, consider another experiment conducted by Paul Rozin regarding how people reason about evil.

Imagine I take out of my closet an old cardboard box. I want to show you something inside the box. I open the box and pull out a sweater. The sweater is old and somewhat ratty. It hasn't been washed. I tell you that I was given this sweater by my grandfather who had an interest in World War II memorabilia. My grandfather acquired this sweater as a part of his collection. This sweater was owned and worn by Hitler. It's from his actual wardrobe. After Hitler's death many former Nazis took mementos from Hitler's life. Apparently, there is a thriving black market trade for authentic artifacts or articles once owned, used, or worn by Hitler. The sweater I'm showing you was worn by Hitler the week before his suicide. It hasn't been washed since. You can still see his sweat stains.

Would you, I ask, like to put the sweater on?

Research has shown that many people refuse to try the sweater on. More, people report discomfort being near or in the same room with the sweater. A wicked fog surrounds the object and we want to avoid contact with it.

What studies like this reveal is that people tend to think about evil as if it were a virus, a disease, or a contagion. Evil is an *object* that can seep out of Hitler, into the sweater, and, by implication, into you if you try the sweater on. Evil is sticky and contagious. So we stay away.

What we see in this example is how disgust psychology regulates how we reason about and experience aspects of the moral universe. Disgust psychology prompts us to think about evil as if it were a virus or a polluting object. When we do this the logic of contamination is imported into moral discourse and judgment. For example, as noted earlier, we begin to worry about *contact*. In the domain of food aversion contact with a polluting object is a legitimate concern. But fears concerning contact might not be appropriate or logical in dealing with moral issues or social groups. Worse, a fear of contact might promote antisocial behavior (e.g., social exclusion) on our part.

The example of Hitler might sound extreme, but consider another study done by Paul Rozin, Maureen Markwith, and Clark McCauley.[3] In this study the researchers observed that many people don't want to wear sweaters previously owned by homosexual persons, or even lie down in the same hotel bed if a homosexual person was the previous night's occupant. In short, just about any behavior judged to be sin could activate disgust psychology, subsequently importing contamination logic (e.g., contact fears) into the life of the church.

We find magical thinking at work in Matthew 9. If sin is "contagious," extending hospitality becomes impossible. This is the psychological dynamic at the heart of the conflict in Matthew 9. What worries the Pharisees is Jesus' *contact* with sinners. This worry over *proximity* is symptomatic of the magical thinking imported into the religious domain through the psychology of disgust.

Let's pause here and update our list of features that characterize disgust psychology. We've already noted the boundary monitoring, expulsive, and promiscuous aspects of disgust. We can now add a fourth feature to our list:

1. *A Boundary Psychology*: Disgust is a system that monitors *boundaries*. Disgust regulates the act of incorporation and inclusion.
2. *Expulsive*: Disgust is a violently *expulsive* mechanism. In mild forms disgust simply prompts *withdrawal* and *avoidance*. In stronger forms disgust involves violent *rejection, expulsion,* or *elimination.*

---

3. Rozin et al., "Sensitivity to Indirect Contacts," 495–505.

3. *Promiscuous*: Due to disgust's developmental peculiarities (i.e., its sensitive period), culture can link disgust to a variety of stimuli, many unrelated to food. Consequently, disgust is often found regulating moral, social, and religious experiences.

4. *Magical Thinking*: The contamination appraisals involved in disgust are characterized by magical thinking, which overrides reason and logic. Consequently, when disgust regulates moral, social, or religious experience magical thinking is unwittingly imported into the life of the church.

3.

The logic of contamination is called "magical" because it makes causal judgments that defy the laws of physics. That isn't to say that magical thinking has no basis in reality or adaptive value. Generally speaking, if a foodstuff makes contact with or is in close physical proximity to a known pollutant we should, from an adaptive stance, be wary about eating the food. Contact is a legitimate heuristic in thinking about contagion and contamination. The problem comes when the logic of "contact" begins to be applied in situations where it shouldn't apply.

To this point we've mainly focused on the notion of contact in contamination judgments. But there are other features of contamination logic that are important to consider in light of the chapters to come. And as with the judgment of contact, each of these aspects of contamination logic is problematic when imported into the moral, social, and religious domains.

I'd like to focus on four principles of contagion as have been described by Paul Rozin and his colleagues:

1. *Contact*: Contamination is caused by contact or physical proximity.
2. *Dose Insensitivity*: Minimal, even micro, amounts of the pollutant confer harm.
3. *Permanence*: Once deemed contaminated nothing can be done to rehabilitate or purify the object.

4. *Negativity Dominance*: When a pollutant and a pure object come into contact the pollutant is "stronger" and ruins the pure object. The pure object doesn't render the pollutant acceptable or palatable.[4]

We've already seen the moral problems caused by the logic of contact. Let's briefly discuss the problems associated with the other facets of contamination logic from our list.

Dose insensitivity is the appraisal that minute amounts of a pollutant will create contamination. That is, the "dose" can be little or large and it doesn't matter. The classic phrase in the literature is, "A drop of urine in a bottle of wine will ruin the bottle of wine. But a drop of wine in a bottle of urine will do nothing to make the urine drinkable."[5] To sharpen this point, imagine a whole swimming pool of clean wine. On the far end you see me drop in a teaspoon of urine. Has the wine in the pool become polluted? Most say yes. Would you drink a bottle of wine from the pool? Probably not.

The point here is that the "logic" of dose insensitivity implies that even very small "pollutants" can have catastrophic effects. As illustrations, consider how dose insensitivity governs how people reason in the following situations:

1. Emotional reactions to small, seemingly insignificant, changes in worship practices.
2. The eliminationist anti-Semitism of the Nazi Final Solution.
3. Neighborhood outrage when a public playground is found to have trace (but harmless) amounts of toxins in the ground soil.

In each of these situations we find that dose insensitivity creates binary judgments. That is, we don't think of something as being "a little" contaminated. "Dosage" is irrelevant. A small amount of contamination doesn't compute. Something either is contaminated or it's not. Consider the examples. In my church tradition small changes to worship practices, seemingly irrelevant, became huge sources of conflict. Like a drop of urine in a bottle of wine the small change— the polluting influence—ruined the acceptability of the worship. Changes to worship were dose insensitive.

4. Rozin et al., "Operation of the Laws," 703–12.
5. Rozin and Fallon, "A Perspective on Disgust," 23–41.

Consider also how dose insensitivity drives the logic of ethnic cleansing. If, as the Nazi's believed, Jews were polluting influences then dose insensitivity demanded complete elimination and extermination. The existence of a single Jew was too much to stand.

Finally, consider how dose insensitivity affects policy. Our world is never hazard free. We are willing to live with some acceptable level of risk. We all, for example, drive cars on the road. But certain social and policy issues activate contamination judgments. When this happens the logic of dose insensitivity is imported into the discussion. For example, how much toxin is tolerable in the groundsoil of a child's playground? Even asking the question seems immoral. The obvious answer, given dose insensitivity logic, is none, zero percent. And yet a "clean up" goal of zero percent might not be physically or economically feasible.

In each of these examples—religious, social, political—we see how dose insensitivity logic can produce dysfunction. And yet few of us are aware of the moment when dose insensitivity logic has been imported into our conversation, framing how we see the world.

Consider next the contamination attribution of *permanence*. The judgment of permanence is characterized by the attribution that once an object becomes contaminated, nothing can be done to rehabilitate the object. Recall the bug in the juice experiments. Once the juice was judged to be contaminated, nothing could be done to rehabilitate the juice, to make it drinkable again. Once polluted, always polluted.

The judgment of permanence will be important in Part 2 when we consider sins that are uniquely structured by purity metaphors. As we will see, when moral infractions are governed by a contamination logic the attribution of permanence—once polluted, always polluted—is imported into the sin experience. Such sins become emotionally traumatic due to the judgment that *permanent, non-rehabilitative ruin* has occurred. As a consequence, these "contamination sins" carry an enormous load of guilt, shame, and self-loathing within the church. After these sins people may "give up," morally speaking, as some "pure" moral state or status has been irrevocably lost or ruined. Think of the way a teenager, motivated by the metaphor of "sexual purity," might respond to the loss of virginity. Or how an alcoholic might respond to "falling off the wagon" with one drink. In light of the attribution of permanence people in these circumstances might just throw in the towel, morally speaking, and continue to have sex or proceed to the next drink. If total ruin has occurred, then, according to the dose insensitivity logic, more of the same isn't going to make anything worse.

Finally, consider the attribute of *negativity dominance*. The judgment of negativity dominance places all the power on the side of the pollutant. If I touch (apologies for the example I'm about to use) some feces to your cheeseburger the cheeseburger gets ruined, permanently (see above). Importantly, the cheeseburger doesn't make the feces suddenly scrumptious. When the pure and the polluted come into contact the pollutant is the more powerful force. The negative dominates over the positive.

Negativity dominance has important missional implications for the church. For example, notice how negativity dominance is at work in Matthew 9. The Pharisees never once consider the fact that the contact between Jesus and the sinners might have a purifying, redemptive, and cleansing effect upon the sinners. Why not? The logic of contamination simply doesn't work that way. The logic of contamination has the power of the negative dominating over the positive. Jesus doesn't purify the sinners. The sinners make Jesus unclean.

Negativity dominance is problematic in the life of the church because, in the missional moment, when the church makes contact with the world, the power sits firmly with the world as the location of impurity. According to the logic of negativity dominance, contact with the world defiles the *church*. Given this logic the only move open to the church is withdrawal and quarantine, separation from the world. In short, many missional failures are simply the product of the church following the intuitive logic of disgust psychology.

What is striking about the gospel accounts is how Jesus reverses negativity dominance. Jesus is, to coin a term, *positivity dominant*. Contact with Jesus purifies. A missional church embraces this reversal, following Jesus into the world without fears of contamination. But it is important to note that this is a deeply counterintuitive position to take. Nothing in our experience suggests that this should be the case. The missional church will always be swimming against the tide of disgust psychology, always tempted to separate, withdraw, and quarantine.

PART 2

Purity

Are you washed in the blood,
In the soul-cleansing blood of the Lamb?
Are your garments spotless? Are they white as snow?
Are you washed in the blood of the Lamb?

—*Are You Washed in the Blood?* by Elisha A. Hoffman (1878)

3

Morality and Metaphors

Out, damned spot! Out, I say!

—Lady Macbeth, *Macbeth*

1.

In Part 1 we reviewed the psychological literature concerning the psychology of disgust. At various points we noted how contamination appraisals and the emotion of disgust often regulate moral affect and judgment, how we experience and reason about right versus wrong. Here in Part 2—*Purity*—we will explore in greater detail the connections between disgust and morality.

To begin, there is a growing consensus that the link between disgust and morality is mediated by metaphor. Much of the pioneering research in this area has been done George Lakoff and Mark Johnson who have brought attention to the metaphorical nature of human cognition.[1] Specifically, Lakoff and Johnson have shown how humans grasp abstractions by grounding them in concrete metaphors. These metaphors are not the poetic or airy metaphors of literature. Rather, these metaphors are largely structured by the human sensorimotor system. As Lakoff and Johnson have argued, cognition is *embodied*. Even our most abstract and philosophical speculations are

1. See Lakoff and Johnson's *Metaphors We Live By* and *Philosophy in the Flesh*

very often grounded in our motor and sensory experiences. For example, why is "up" generally good and "down" generally bad? The mapping of up/good and down/bad isn't arbitrary. The experience of our bodies biases us toward this mapping. The experience of illness, fatigue, sleep, and death are associated with the body lying *down*. Conversely, the experience of life, vigor, wakefulness, and health is associated with standing *up*. These sensorimotor experiences bias the mind toward the metaphor Up = Good and Down = Bad. Although there is no logical rationale for this mapping, and any given culture could reverse the metaphor, the Up = Good and Down = Bad metaphor is psychologically intuitive and appealing as it is grounded in universal experiences with the body. Once a valence is mapped onto the vertical dimension we see the metaphor applied across diverse domains. For example, in many faith systems hell is "down" in the bowels of the earth (an *under*world) and heaven is "up" and above the earth. Outside of theology we see the Up/Good and Down/Bad in domains such as health (e.g., He's *down* with the flu), power (e.g., You want to move *up* in this company), mood (e.g., I'm feeling *up* today), and morality (e.g., He's a *low-down* person).

Given the critical role metaphors play in human cognition, particularly the way embodied metaphors ground abstractions, it is no surprise that the biblical writers use a wide variety of metaphors to describe the Christian experience. Our particular focus concerns those metaphors that help Christians reason about the moral domain. Generally speaking, these are soteriological metaphors, the metaphors used to approach the experiences of sin and grace. To grasp the diversity of the soteriological metaphors, consider a partial listing of Sin/Grace metaphors used in the New Testament (see Table 1):

Table 1

Selected List of Sin and Grace Metaphors in the New Testament

Metaphor	Sin	Salvation/Grace	Textual Example
Purity	Contaminated/Dirty	Pure/Clean	Heb 10:22
Rescue	Perishing	Saved	2 Cor 2:15
Economic	Debt	Payment	Matt 18:27

Metaphor	Sin	Salvation/Grace	Textual Example
Legal	Crime and Punishment	Forgiveness/ Justification	Rev 18:5
Freedom	Slavery	Emancipation	1 Cor 7:23
Optics	Dark	Light	John 1:5
Seeking	Lost	Found	Luke 15
Nation	Alien	Citizen	Eph 2:19
Health	Illness	Health	Matt 9:12
Relational	Enemy	Friend	Jas 4:4
Military	War	Peace	2 Cor 10:4
Epistemology	Ignorance	Knowledge	Luke 11:52
Familial	Orphan	Adoption	Eph 1:5
Horticultural	Pruned	Grafted in	Rom 11:24
Vision	Blindness	Sight	Matt 15:14
Development	Infancy	Maturity	1 Pet 2:2
Biological	Death	Life	Rom 6:23
Ambulatory	Falling/ Stumbling	Standing/ Walking	1 Cor 15:58
Truth	Error/False	Correct/True	Gal 2:4
Performance	Lose	Win	Phil 3:14
Sleep	Sleep	Awake	Mark 13:36
Captive	Hostage	Ransom	Heb 9:15

Many of these metaphors are embodied, intimately associated with the experiences of our physical bodies: falling down, sleeping, seeing, growing up, illness, death. Other metaphors are more social, grounded in the day-to-day experience of community: family, friendship, citizenry. As can be seen in Table 1, the experience of grace is very rich, unable to be captured by or reduced to a single metaphor. Rather, each metaphor provides a window, a bounded perspective that provides partial illumination of a much larger phenomenon.

As Lakoff and Johnson have shown, these metaphors help us structure and reason about abstract concepts. Each metaphor comes with specific entailments, implications that are intuitively suggested by the dominant metaphor. These entailments create a "logic" that is governed and made available by the metaphor. This metaphorical logic is what grants us cognitive traction, a means to reason through complex problems or abstractions. For example, if a relationship is "broken" the natural entailment of this metaphor is that the relationship might be "fixed." I've chosen this example as it nicely illustrates how metaphors come with certain entailments (e.g., what is "broken" might be "fixed") and how those entailments might obscure as much as they illuminate. For example, although we might say a relationship is "broken" is it accurate to expect that a relationship can be "fixed" as one would fix a car? In short, the broken/fixed metaphor might be too optimistic and mechanistic a metaphor for approaching relational reconciliation. Further, the broken/fixed metaphor can also entail a judgment of blame. Who broke the relationship? The metaphor starts nudging us in unhelpful directions.

The point is that metaphors can distort as much as they illuminate. No doubt this is why the biblical writers deploy a diversity of metaphors in approaching the experience of grace. And yet it is often the case that certain metaphors can come to dominate the conversation about grace and sin. Not only does this represent a loss of complexity, but it should also cause us to wonder about the entailments associated with the dominant metaphors. As noted above, these entailments can hide as much as they reveal. And without countervailing metaphors in play the distortions inherent in a given metaphor can affect the life and mission of the church. Obviously, our concern will be with the purity metaphors in soteriological discussions and the entailments they import into the life of the church. We'll discuss why these metaphors naturally come to dominate, bias, and eventually distort the experiences of sin and salvation.

2.

As seen in Table 1 the experiences of sin and grace within Christianity are often framed by purity/pollution and clean/unclean metaphors. These are embodied metaphors that help us understand sin and grace by appealing to the experience of disgust, our daily experiences with dirt, filth, water, hygiene, food, feces, contamination, pollution, and washing. Given these associations, cleanliness and purity are identified as good, as the location of grace. Dirt and uncleanliness are identified as bad, as locations of sin and moral pollution.

In the biblical witness, purity metaphors are rooted in the Levitical purity codes that governed the communal and cultic life of Israel. In

Leviticus, Yahweh outlines procedures for handling a variety of potential contaminants in the life of Israel: food (Leviticus 11), infectious skin diseases (Leviticus 13–14), mildew (Leviticus 13–14), childbirth (Leviticus 12), menstrual blood and bodily discharges (Leviticus 15), hygiene (Leviticus 13–14), and sexual activity (Leviticus 18). In many of these cases the "impurity" is real, a legitimate source of disease that the community needed to manage. But the concern over "cleanliness" was also imported as a metaphor into the sociomoral domain, regulating the moral and spiritual life of Israel. Moral failings—sins—were also considered to be "pollutants" and sources of impurity.

This metaphor comes with certain entailments. Defense against dirt and contamination demands washing and acts of strict quarantine. Consequently, in Leviticus Yahweh outlines purification procedures through sacrifices, washings, and offerings to manage and "clean up" these social and moral contaminants. What is striking is all this is how powerfully *bodily* experiences structured how the *spiritual* facets of life were to be managed. A physical washing was understood to effect a spiritual cleansing. The physical washing was not, as we might expect, symbolic; it was literal and causal. Further, similar to how one would handle contagious disease, zones of quarantine were also established in the life of Israel, holy places set apart from workaday existence. What we see in all this is how the purity metaphor imports certain entailments into the moral and spiritual life of Israel. Physical washing is found to be spiritually sanitizing. Quarantine is the means to produce a state or location of holiness. No doubt purity metaphors communicated a deep spiritual truth, that sin in the life of Israel was a profound danger that needed to be dealt with. Perhaps no metaphor captures the malevolent invasive danger of sin as well as purity metaphors. And yet the various entailments of purity metaphors, driven by the dynamics of disgust psychology reviewed in Part 1, may create problems if they come to dominate the soteriological experience of the church.

Purity metaphors also run through the New Testament, mainly due to the fact that the early church saw sacrificial themes in the death of Jesus. Specifically, the Day of Atonement ritual in Leviticus became a significant metaphor for how the church came to understand its own experience of salvation. On the Day of Atonement, as described in Leviticus 16, the "uncleanness of the Israelites" (v. 19) was purified through a blood sacrifice and the scapegoating ritual. The governing metaphor of the Day of Atonement was cleansing/purification: "because on this day atonement will be made for you, to cleanse you. Then, before the Lord, you will be clean from all your sins" (v. 30). In the New Testament the blood of Jesus also performs this sanitizing function, "washing away sin." As Paul says in 1 Corinthians 6:

> Do you not know that the wicked will not inherit the kingdom of God? . . . And that is what some of you were. But you were washed, you were sanctified, you were justified in the name of the Lord Jesus Christ and by the Spirit of our God.

Consequently, it is not surprising that the central salvation ritual of the Christian church—baptism—is a physical washing in water. The conflation of moral and physical washing observed in baptism is nicely captured in Heb 10:22:

> Let us draw near to God with a sincere heart in full assurance of faith, having our hearts sprinkled to cleanse us from a guilty conscience and having our bodies washed with pure water.

The book of Revelation also depicts the saints who "have washed their robes and made them white in the blood of the Lamb." This image, the cleansing power of Christ's blood, became a recurring image in Christian hymnody. I still remember, as a child, singing the song *Nothing But the Blood*:

> What can wash away my sin?
> Nothing but the blood of Jesus;
> What can make me whole again?
> Nothing but the blood of Jesus.
>
> For my pardon, this I see,
> Nothing but the blood of Jesus;
> For my cleansing this my plea,
> Nothing but the blood of Jesus.
>
> Oh! precious is the flow
> That makes me white as snow;
> No other fount I know,
> Nothing but the blood of Jesus.

Of course, washing isn't the only metaphor for Christian baptism. The Apostle Paul, for example, compares Christian baptism to a burial. This metaphor places resurrection (life), rather than purity, at the center of the salvation experience. But it is clear that purity is a central way Christians, both ancient and modern, have come to understand the experience of sin and grace. Sin is dirt, being morally unclean. Salvation is being pure, washed as "white as snow."

3.

None of this is particularly worrisome if it were not for the fact that some Christian communities come to privilege certain metaphors over others. This is to be expected, as some metaphors are more common in Scripture. As we have noted, the metaphor of salvation as being clean, washed, or pure is ubiquitous in both the Old and New Testaments. However, if we are not careful a small handful of privileged metaphors can come to dominate the faith experience of the church. When this happens the rich complexity of the salvation experience (see Table 1) is lost or occluded. Salvation becomes reduced, perhaps unwittingly, to the mechanisms entailed by a single metaphor. This is troublesome as metaphors, being metaphors, distort as much as they reveal. While the core entailments of a metaphor help us understand the experience of salvation, other entailments inherent in the metaphor can produce theological confusion. When we push past the core entailments of a metaphor we begin to suspect that the metaphor, to use a metaphor, has been "stretched too far."

Consider the debates going on in churches and theological circles regarding the dominance of penal substitutionary atonement in many Christian communities. This soteriological system is so common that I doubt I need to review the relevant details. The core feature of the doctrine, in compressed form, is that Jesus "substitutes" himself for sinners on the cross, taking upon himself the punishment of sin. Further, as noted above, the sacrificial shedding of Christ's blood—seen as a perfect and, thus, final sin-offering—washes, cleanses or "covers" the sins of believers. These are two of the metaphors that regulate the "logic" of penal substitutionary atonement. The first is a crime and punishment metaphor (hence the word "penal"). The "substitution" involves Jesus accepting the punishment for our crimes (sins) against God. The second metaphor is the one that concerns us: the notion of purity, that the blood of Jesus "washes sins away." The purity metaphor often regulates how Christians understand the doctrine of "imputed righteousness," the idea that the righteousness of Jesus is given over or reckoned to the believer. The believer stands in a location of filth and contamination and is fundamentally unable to become "clean." Anything humans touch subsequently becomes contaminated. Only the sacrifice of Jesus can "save" us, wash us clean. Thus, any holiness, purity, righteousness, or sanctity found with the believer is the sole product of Christ's salvific work. To be clear, there are other metaphors that help Christians think through the doctrine of imputed righteousness. These are often economic metaphors: metaphors of reckoning, exchange, gift-giving, and debt. But purity metaphors generally dominate as they link the sacrificial (blood shedding) aspects of the Hebrew Day of Atonement with the bloody death of Jesus on Calvary.

The concern over the ascendancy and dominance of penal substitutionary atonement in many sectors of Christianity is the concern expressed above, that the salvation experience is being reduced to the handful of metaphors that govern penal substitutionary thinking. The worry is that an over-reliance on the penal substitutionary metaphors is leading to a loss of complexity and nuance within the Christian community. More, there is a worry that the entailments of the regulating metaphors behind penal substitutionary atonement are being pushed too far, that the "logic" of these metaphors is being taken too literally, creating confused and thin understandings of sin and grace.

What are some of the concerns regarding the penal substitutionary metaphors? Some of this debate is theological and exegetical, often centering upon Paul and the proper understanding of his doctrine of justification. Specifically, some suggest that the penal substitutionary metaphors, read too literally, create a problematic view of God: that God is inherently a God of retributive justice who can only be "satisfied" with blood sacrifice. A more missional worry is that the metaphors behind penal substitutionary atonement reduce salvation to a binary status: Justified versus Condemned and Pure versus Impure. The concern is that when salvation reduces to avoiding the judgment of God (Jesus accepting our "death sentence") and accepting Christ's righteousness as our own (being "washed" and made "holy" for the presence of God), we can ignore the biblical teachings that suggest that salvation is communal, cosmic in scope, and is an ongoing developmental process. These understandings of atonement—that salvation is an active communal engagement that participates in God's cosmic mission to restore all things—are vital to efforts aimed at motivating spiritual formation and missional living. As many have noted, by ignoring the communal, cosmic, and developmental facets of salvation penal substitutionary atonement becomes individualistic and pietistic. The central concern of penal substitutionary atonement is standing "washed" and "justified" before God. No doubt there is an individual aspect to salvation—every metaphor has a bit of the truth—but restricting our view to the legal and purity metaphors blinds us to the fact that atonement has developmental, social, political, and ecological implications.

4.

I've brought up these concerns regarding penal substitutionary atonement because purity metaphors are deeply implicated in the doctrine. Consequently, I'd like to consider how the psychology behind these purity metaphors might shed some light on the contemporary debates regarding penal substitutionary atonement. First, why is penal substitutionary thinking so ubiquitous? What makes these metaphors so attractive, appealing, and powerful? And why is this doctrine so hard to dislodge? Second, do these metaphors really attenuate missional engagement? Can the experience of feeling "saved," "washed," and "pure" really cause a person to disengage, missionally speaking, from the world?

Let's first consider why penal substitutionary thinking is so appealing.

Recall the sweet tooth metaphor from the opening chapter. Why is penal substitutionary thinking so widespread, so appealing, and so resistant to nuance? No doubt history played a decisive role in this story, but certain psychological dynamics have also been involved. And these psychological dynamics have made penal substitutionary thinking, once it arrived on the theological stage during the Reformation, both attractive and intuitive. Some ideas, to use a term from Malcolm Gladwell's book *The Tipping Point*, are more or less "sticky," psychologically speaking: more likely to stick in the mind and be shared with others. For example, the psychologists Chip Heath, Chris Bell, and Emily Sternberg have suggested that ideas and stories undergo what they call "emotional selection" within a community, a term meant to conjure up Darwin's notion of natural selection.[2] According to Heath, Bell, and Sternberg, ideas and stories become "selected" (i.e., remembered and transmitted) when they "evoke an emotional reaction that is shared across people." Emotion, we all know, is intimately involved in memory. Moments of joy or experiences of burning shame are hard to forget. In their research Heath, Bell, and Sternberg manipulated the emotional salience of various urban legends and found that more emotionally powerful stories underwent an emotional selection. The researchers were successful in making stories more "sticky," more likely to be remembered and shared with others. Interestingly, the emotional variable Heath, Bell, and Sternberg manipulated was disgust. This is the same psychology sitting behind the purity metaphors found in penal substitutionary atonement.

In short, one reason penal substitutionary atonement might be so popular is that it is sticky; it activates an emotional system that makes its metaphors highly memorable and, thus, more likely to be shared in the activities of evangelism, testimony, or catechesis. Penal substitutionary atonement might be a theological sweet tooth.

What makes these metaphors so "sweet," so psychologically sticky? Recent psychological research suggests that the psychological connection between salvation and washing might be innate. If so, this might be the reason for why penal substitutionary atonement is so attractive and ubiquitous as a doctrine. The innate embodied associations between purity and salvation make the penal substitutionary metaphors psychologically sticky: more memorable, intuitive, evocative, and, thus, more likely to be transmitted on to others. The metaphors "fit" the mind, so to speak. Building on our sweet tooth metaphor we might say that the metaphors of penal substitutionary

2. Heath et al., "Emotional Selection in Memes," 1028–41.

atonement make it a kind of theological "junk food": appealing and alluring, but problematic if overindulged. One needs a balanced theological diet.

What is the evidence for this deep psychological link between purity, disgust, morality, and salvation? Consider three studies conducted by Chen-Bo Zhong and Katie Liljenquist about what they call *The Macbeth Effect*.[3] The Macbeth Effect, named for Lady Macbeth who tries to wash away her guilt through hand washing, is the psychological tendency to link physical cleansing with moral cleansing. What we see in Lady Macbeth is another form of magical thinking, the belief that *physical* washing has a *causal* effect in *moral* purification. The link here between physical and spiritual washing isn't simply *symbolic* (i.e., the physical washing *symbolizes* the spiritual transformation) but *causal* (i.e., the physical washing *effects* the spiritual cleansing).

Do normal people reason about moral infractions like Lady Macbeth? Yes they do. In the first of the three studies, Zhong and Liljenquist divided participants into one of two groups: a control condition and a condition where the participants were asked to imagine moral infractions they had committed in the past. Obviously, by having participants recall past sins the goal was to have them revisit and experience moments of shame and guilt. After this exercise the participants in both groups were asked to engage in a word completion task. The incomplete words could be completed in a cleansing or non-cleansing fashion. For example, the stimulus "S O __ P" could be filled in as either "SOUP" (a non-cleansing response) or "SOAP" (a cleansing response). Psychologists use word completion tasks like this to examine the associative networks in human cognition. For example, if moral infractions are unrelated to physical cleansing then there should be no reason why the participants who imagined past sins should complete the words any differently than the control participants. But if sins are psychologically associated with physical cleansing then we would expect that, relative to controls, the participants who imagined past sins would be more likely to write "SOAP" rather than "SOUP." That is, imagining moral failures activated notions associated with physical cleaning. This is, in fact, what Zhong

3. Zhong and Liljenquist, "Washing Away Your Sins," 1451–52.

and Liljenquist observed. When compared to control participants, people who had revisited their moral failures were more likely to recall cleansing-related words. In short, *sin* makes us think about *dirt*.

In a follow-up study the participants were offered a token gift, either a pencil or an antiseptic wipe. In a finding supportive of the word-completion results, participants who were asked to recall their past sins were more likely, relative to control participants, to choose the antiseptic wipe over the pencil. Taken together, these findings suggest that being exposed to your *moral failings* stimulated a need for *physical cleansing*. When we *sin* we like to take *showers*. We all act like Lady Macbeth.

It appears, then, that the morality/cleansing link isn't simply a religious artifact. Rather, like the Up/Down metaphor discussed at the start of this chapter, the morality/cleansing metaphor is deeply rooted in the life of the body, in this case our primitive experiences with dirt, water, and hygiene. As they say, cleanliness is next to godliness.

What all this suggests is that humans naturally reason about morality, sin, and salvation through the embodied metaphors of purity and cleanliness, the metaphors deeply embedded in penal substitutionary doctrines. It seems we can't help but think of sin in terms of dirt and contamination. In fact, dirt and cleanliness might be the primal and foundational metaphor of sin and salvation, the psychotheological bedrock upon which subsequent understandings are built. In all this we find salvation-as-purity to be a theological sweet tooth, an innate and embodied metaphor that can pull theological reflection into its orbit and occasionally, like a black hole, completely "capture" and "collapse" soteriological thinking, reducing notions of salvation down to a metaphorical singularity.

5.

The presence of purity metaphors in penal substitutionary atonement might explain why the doctrine is so psychologically and theologically appealing. We have, as the research of Zhong and Liljenquist suggests, a natural inclination to think of salvation in terms of purity and cleanliness. But so what? Beyond making penal substitutionary thinking appealing, why is this association problematic? Recall, one of the concerns regarding the penal substitutionary metaphors is that they might attenuate missional engagement. Feeling "saved" and "clean" we lose missional motivation and downplay the biblical injunctions that suggest that salvation is an ongoing process of sanctification and, following the Greek Orthodox tradition, theosis: The gradual process of being formed into the image of Christ.

But is this true? Do purity metaphors cause us to become morally lax and self-satisfied? The answer appears to be yes.

Recall, again, the research on the Macbeth Effect. If a causal link is made (via magical thinking) between physical purity and moral purity then it is only a short step to think that physical cleansing can *replace* moral righteousness. That is, if the physical cleansing *causes* moral cleansing, then, it stands to reason, *moral purity can be achieved through physical washing*. This is the Macbeth Effect, the belief that *physical* cleansing creates *moral* purity.

In the gospels the Macbeth Effect was a point of contention between Jesus and the Pharisees. In Matthew 15, Jesus and the Pharisees debate the purity ritual of washing hands before eating. Jesus makes a clear distinction between physical cleansing and moral behavior, noting that hand washing does not make a person "clean" or "unclean," morally speaking. Rather, it is what "proceeds from the heart" (Jesus lists behaviors such as murder, theft, and adultery) that defiles a person.

Now you might think that modern people would be immune to the religious superstition that mere hand washing absolves you of moral responsibility. But you would be wrong. Specifically, in the third of their three studies Zhong and Liljenquist went on to examine this replacement effect (that physical cleansing replaces moral responsibility). In this study participants were once again asked to recall a moral failure. Afterward, some participants were allowed to use an antiseptic wipe. After using the wipe (or not) the participants were asked to give mood ratings. Many of the mood ratings assessed moral emotions: disgust, regret, shame, guilt. After the mood ratings the participants were also asked to engage in an act of helpful volunteerism (participating for another study without pay to help out a desperate graduate student).

What did Zhong and Liljenquist find? They observed two things. First, if participants were allowed to use an antiseptic wipe after recalling a moral failure they were less helpful. Where 74 percent of the control participants agreed to help out the graduate student, only 41 percent of those who used a wipe agreed to assist. Second, when compared to controls, those using the antiseptic wipe reported fewer negative moral emotions (e.g., less shame, less guilt) after recalling their moral failure. In short, the Macbeth Effect was in force. The physical act of washing made people feel *less guilty* and *reduced their willingness to engage in an altruistic act.* Physical cleansing replaced morality, both emotionally and behaviorally. Physical washing makes people feel morally cleaner and, seemingly, morally self-satisfied to the point of unhelpfulness. You already feel like a good person so why do *more* good?

This laboratory research suggests that the behavior of the Pharisees in the gospels was not unusual. It would appear that the Macbeth Effect is a ubiquitous phenomenon, a product of human psychology rather than religious superstition. The reason for this seems to be the deep and embodied association between purity and morality. The two are so closely associated in the human mind that one can, as illogical as it might sound, stand in the place of the other.

And this is, as we have discussed, the pastoral worry about penal substitutionary atonement. It is the concern that once the status of saved is obtained the believer loses missional motivation. Being found "clean," there is little left for the believer to do. The psychic experience of being "saved" and "washed clean by the blood of Jesus" can function like those antiseptic wipes in Zhong and Liljenquist's research—soothing the conscience and, as a consequence, reducing prosocial motivation. This is the pietistic temptation, seeking a personal experience of "cleansing" at the expense of social and political engagement. The spiritual experience of being pure replaces passionate moral effort.

These psychological dynamics help illuminate the events in Matthew 9, the tension between mercy and sacrifice. And it also explains why this tension will be a constant and consistent temptation in the life of the church. In the actions of the Pharisees we see how the experience of purity (the sacrificial impulse) had come to replace morality (the mercy impulse). In light of Zhong and Liljenquist's research it seems that everyone, religious and irreligious alike, is prone to this mistake. In sum, although the experience of purity helps us understand morality, the metaphorical connection between the two is so deep that the experience of physical purity can come to replace moral action. And, given that the church is awash in purity metaphors, particularly those churches who privilege penal substitutionary thinking, there exists a constant danger that the church will exchange the private *experience* of salvation, being washed in the blood of the Lamb, for passionate missional *engagement* with the world.

6.

We have been discussing how purity metaphors often structure *general* notions of sin and salvation, keeping an eye on the social, psychological, and missional consequences of those metaphors. But before concluding this chapter I'd like for us to also consider how purity metaphors, with their associated contamination logic, can structure our experience of *particular* sin categories. I hope to show that purity metaphors are often deployed unevenly across the sin domains, and how this imbalance goes a fair distance in explaining some ecclesial and pastoral puzzles.

When you attend to the sin metaphors in churches you notice that many, if not most, sin categories are governed by performance and ambulatory metaphors. Sins are "failures," "mistakes," "falling short," "getting lost," or "falling down." Recall that metaphors have entailments, an inferential logic that governs how we reason about abstractions. These performance and ambulatory metaphors have rehabilitative entailments. If a person makes a "mistake" she can "try again." If we get "lost" we can "get back on the straight and narrow path." If we "stumble" we can "stand up" again.

If you listen closely in churches, these performance and ambulatory metaphors structure how many Christians reason about and experience a wide variety of moral infractions from lying to lust. What is important to notice is how the rehabilitative entailments of these metaphors make the emotional and behavioral movement toward repentance and confession easy and intuitive. Just make the choice to "try again."

In short, although sin is, generically speaking, understood to be a purity violation, few sins are *specifically* regulated by purity metaphors. In fact, in my experience only one sin category—sexual sin— is almost uniquely and universally regulated by purity metaphors, often with toxic effect.

Although churches routinely teach that "all sins are equally offensive" to God (i.e., every sin is a purity violation) certain sins are often experienced as more shameful and produce more intense self-loathing and guilt. Some of this has to do with issues of severity. For example, murder is more severe than stealing paper clips from work. This, in itself, shows some of the inadequacy of purity metaphors in regulating the notion of God's holiness. Consider, for example, the notion that "all *crimes* are equal." The idea is nonsensical. Not buckling your seatbelt isn't the moral equivalent of murder. Thus, the "all *sins* are equal" formulation only makes sense given the background entailments of purity logic. Specifically, "all sins are equal" is the purity entailment of dose insensitivity, the notion that just a drop of urine ruins the barrel of wine. Thus, even a "minor" sin contaminates the holiness of God. Sin "dosage" is irrelevant if a purity metaphor is regulating notions of holiness. And like all metaphors, the dose insensitivity entailment of "all sins are equal" distorts the nature of sin as much as it illuminates.

Beyond issues of severity, some sins are unique loci of shame as they are almost universally regulated by purity metaphors. As noted above, in my experience these are almost always the sexual sins. As many are aware, sexual sins are often experienced in faith communities as being a class unto themselves, as a particular location of stigma and shame. Why might this be? One answer is that sexuality is distinct among sin categories in being almost uniquely regulated by a purity metaphor. Talk of "sexual purity" is common in most churches. In contrast, few other moral categories are regulated by purity metaphors. We don't speak of materialism or truth-telling as forms of "purity." When we spend impulsively or tell a lie we think of these as performance errors—mistakes—rather than as a loss of a virginal moral purity. No doubt there are good reasons for using purity categories to regulate sexual behavior. By the time we are adolescents any "purity" we might have had in regard to honesty has long since been lost. But virginity is very often carried into adolescence and, thus, is able to be understood as a state of "purity" that can be "lost." But this still does not explain why sexual sins are considered to be more shameful. No doubt a lot of it has to do with the gravity of the social consequences surrounding pregnancy. In Part 4 of this book we'll dig deeper into the connections between disgust, purity, and sexuality. Regardless, it seems clear that both church and society appear to apply to sexuality the most powerful, in regards to stigma, of its regulating metaphors.

But why are purity metaphors such a source of stigma, shame, and guilt? A part of the answer has to do with the possibility of rehabilitation. Recall, most sin categories are structured by metaphors that entail rehabilitation. But purity metaphors have no such entailments. Recall that contamination judgments are governed by the attribution of permanence. Once a foodstuff is judged to be polluted or contaminated nothing can be done to rehabilitate the situation. The fly in the soup ruins it. Consequently, when sins are structured by purity metaphors there is no obvious route to repentance. The metaphor only entails permanent defilement and ruin. And this is, incidentally, the experience of sexual sin. The feeling of a loss that can never be recovered.

There are emotional differences as well. Performance metaphors often entail anger. Frustration, failing to meet a goal, is a universal trigger for anger. And anger, righteously focused, can often be put to good use. By contrast, purity metaphors trigger disgust. When directed at the self this produces self-loathing, shame, and guilt. These emotions are much more difficult to get moving in a positive direction, mainly because they prompt social concealment that thwarts transparency and confession.

In short, purity metaphors, by activating disgust and notions of non-rehabilitation, are some of the most powerful metaphors used to regulate behavior. That is the good news about purity metaphors: they erect strong emotional and behavioral taboos that can be harnessed by moral communities. The bad news is that once the taboo is violated, the offender is crushed by the emotions (self-loathing prompting social concealment) and entailments (permanent, non-rehabilitative ruin) of purity violations. This is very often the experience of sexual sin within many churches.

To be clear, I am not suggesting that sexuality shouldn't be regulated by purity metaphors. I am only attempting to illuminate the psychological and social aspects of various moral metaphors and suggesting that churches pay attention to the effects these metaphors can have upon people. All *sins* might be equal, but all *metaphors* are not. And many of these metaphors create thorny pastoral problems as we engage in spiritual formation efforts within the church.

4

Divinity and Dumbfounding

> O, my offense is rank, it smells to heaven.
>
> —Claudius, *Hamlet*

1.

In the last chapter we discussed how morality is often regulated by purity metaphors, which in turn activates aspects of disgust psychology. However, Christians are by no means consistent in how they deploy purity metaphors. Some Christians may use purity metaphors to structure the entirety of the religious experience, so that everything from morality to doctrine to worship is regulated by notions of purity and contamination. By contrast, other Christians might rarely, if ever, deploy purity metaphors. As a consequence, Christian persons and communities will vary in the degree to which disgust psychology is shaping the spiritual experience, individually and collectively.

This observation is important as the use of purity metaphors is a source of conflict in both the church and in political discourse. The cause of the conflict is twofold. First, there may be a fundamental disagreement about whether or not purity is a legitimate metaphor for a particular moral issue. Consider again the conflict in Matthew 9. The Pharisees approach the situation (Jesus eating with tax collectors and sinners) with a purity metaphor. And as we saw in Part 1, negativity dominance is an entailment of purity logic. Consequently, for the

51

Pharisees the "logic" of the situation is that *Jesus* becomes polluted by his association with sinners. It never occurs to the Pharisees, because it goes against the grain of the regulating purity metaphor, that contact with Jesus might "cleanse" the sinners (what we called "positivity dominance"). That isn't how purity and defilement "work." Jesus, by contrast, rejects the purity metaphor and frames his fellowship with tax collectors as a case of mercy, not sacrifice.

What is being illustrated in Matthew 9 is the mutual incomprehensibility that can occur when individuals disagree about the applicability or appropriateness of purity metaphors. Using the purity metaphor the Pharisees see the situation one way. We, standing with Jesus and eschewing the metaphor, see the situation very differently. Moreover, we come to the exact opposite conclusion. The Pharisees, seeking purity, *pull away* from the sinners. This action is consistent with purity entailments (disgust is an expulsive psychology). Jesus, seeking fellowship, *moves toward* the sinners. One group frames the issue of table fellowship as an issue of *purity*, the sacrificial impulse. The other group frames the issue as one of *mercy*. And, thus, a religious disagreement, with important missional implications, emerges.

The point, obviously, is that religious populations can examine the same moral or social situation and come to radically different judgments depending upon the metaphor they are using to understand the situation. What seems perfectly reasonable and righteous on the inside of the metaphor can seem confused and unjust from the outside.

The second problem with purity metaphors is that not only are these metaphors sources of conflict, the use of these metaphors shuts down conversation altogether. Purity metaphors, as we will see, provide us with few resources for normative adjudication. Not only do these metaphors cause conflict, they also leave us collectively flummoxed with how to move forward in the face of disagreements about normative matters.

In short, if the last chapter discussed the various ways purity metaphors create psychological problems (e.g., the Macbeth Effect) this chapter will discuss how purity metaphors create social and communal problems. We will begin with a discussion of how purity metaphors create conflict and conclude the chapter with a discussion of how purity metaphors thwart conversation and normative adjudication.

2.

Our communal difficulties regarding purity metaphors are due largely to how purity metaphors and disgust psychology come to regulate our collective experiences of the holy, the divine, and the sacred. More specifically, our conceptions of the sacred affect our normative judgments about issues related to dignity, decorum, respect, propriety, and reverence—the attitudes and behaviors we feel are appropriate in the presence of the holy, revered, and sacred.

The psychologist Richard Shweder has argued that cultures structure their lives by deploying three moral grammars, which he labels autonomy, community, and divinity.[1] The ethic of autonomy is sensitive to violations of independence and self-determination. Very often these are limitations upon freedom, the violation of individual rights or harm. Core values of the ethic of autonomy are freedom, choice, safety, and rights. The ethic of community is sensitive to failures of duty, cooperation, or solidarity with the group. Core values of the ethic of community are duty, role-obligation, loyalty, preservation of community, and compliance with authority and norms. Generally speaking, according to Shweder, the ethics of community and autonomy regulate the plane of human interactions in both the social and political realms. And cultures strike different balances between the two ethics. Some cultures value autonomy over community while other cultures value group solidarity over personal freedom.

Our concern here is with the third dimension in Shweder's model, the divinity ethic, the ethic that regulates our interactions with the sacred. The divinity ethic is sensitive to disrespect for or degradation of the sacred found in God, human dignity, or the order of creation. Core values of the divinity ethic are purity, sanctity, propriety, and dignity.

It is important to note that even secular cultures honor a divinity ethic. Outside of the religious sphere there are sacred moments, symbols, places, and rituals. In secular cultures the sacred is often tied up with the national mythology, rituals of statehood, memorials, and places of sacrifice. I recall, as a boisterous Pennsylvanian, being asked by a Texas Ranger to remove my hat and lower my voice on my

1. Shweder et al., "'Big Three' of Morality," 119–69.

first visit to the Alamo in San Antonio, Texas. The place was sacred to Texans and, thus, governed by the ethic of divinity, demanding a sense of decorum, respect, and propriety. Obviously, religious persons understand the ethic of divinity very well, being well versed within their religious traditions in how one encounters the divine through worship and ritual. The point in all this is that many of our normative judgments are driven by divinity ethic violations. Whenever we are offended by a lack of propriety, solemnity, reverence, or dignity the divinity ethic is operative. The divinity ethic also regulates our judgments related to degradation, desecration, the profane, the illicit, and the sacrilegious.[2]

But it might not yet be obvious how purity and disgust come to regulate aspects of the divinity ethic. Notions of the sacred, the divine, and the holy are frequently regulated by a compound metaphor. The first, obviously, is a purity metaphor where notions of holiness are regulated by the entailments of contamination. As with foodstuffs, attributions of pollution/contamination are made when something "clean" comes into contact with a pollutant, the proverbial fly in the soup. In a similar way, the holy and sacred becomes desecrated or profane if it comes into contact with something base and lowly. Thus, in many religious traditions great care is taken to keep the holy and the profane *separated*, hence the notion that what is holy is that which is "set apart" from the common things of the world. This creates the sacred spaces, objects, persons, and rituals of religious life. With purity being the regulating metaphor, holiness requires *quarantine*. Consequently, being built atop disgust psychology, notions of holiness are sensitive to issues of contact between that which is deemed clean and that which is a source of contamination. Recall that disgust is a boundary psychology. Consequently, holiness is at root an issue of boundary monitoring, the separation of the sacred and the profane. The goal is to monitor this boundary and to prevent illicit contact, to keep the holy segregated from the profane. This separation is often accomplished through prohibition and taboo. Further, any movement from the world into the holy will involve acts and rituals of cleansing, purification, and absolution. Nothing "impure" can be carried into the sacred (pure/clean) space.

2. Rozin et al., "CAD Hypothesis," 574–86.

As Mary Douglas notes in her book *Purity and Danger*, "sacred things and places are to be protected from defilement. Holiness and impurity are at opposite poles."[3]

The second metaphor regulating the divinity ethic is an orientational Up/Down metaphor. In this compound metaphor purity becomes associated with "up" and contamination is associated with "down." In short, a distinction between purity and holiness is that holiness often implies *movement* along a vertical dimension. Implicit in notions of holiness is that the holy is "higher" and "heavenly," separated from what is "earthly" and "common." Desecration occurs when something "high" is brought "low." Desecration and degradation involve a movement *downward*. This movement is often triggered by the contamination appraisal, when contact is made between the holy and the profane. Holiness, then, is a conflation of two metaphors, a purity metaphor (pure/polluted) mapped onto a spatial metaphor (up/down). What is holy is not only *pure* but *higher*, an object of the "heavens." What is profane is dirty and of the "earth."

Again, it is important to note that all cultures work with a divinity ethic. As we have just seen, the divinity ethic involves a sense of elevation. This elevation has both a transcendent and a prophylactic function. Specifically, rituals of holiness and purification allow humans to approach the sacred. These rituals are associated with an "upward" experience—spiritual transcendence and our approach of the divine. Prophylactically, the divinity ethic keeps humanity from sliding downward into the bestial, animalistic, or savage. Humans are metaphorically understood to be in between heaven and earth. Humans are "above" the beasts while also being, in the language of the bible, a "little lower than the angels." This notion of humans being "in-between" the bestial and the angelic is nicely captured in the iconic Great Chain of Being, the metaphor that dominated the imaginations of the ancients and still shapes modern understandings of what it means to be human in relation to the animal kingdom, where the bestial, atavistic, and "primitive" are understood to be failures of human dignity, a movement *down* the Great Chain of Being toward the animals.[4]

3. Douglas, *Purity and Danger*, 9.
4. Haidt, "Moral Amplification," 322–35.

In short, the divinity ethic allows humans to approach the divine (allowing movement *upward*) while also protecting human dignity, the sacredness of the human person, and humane society (preventing movement *downward*). If we see a human person naked or urinating in public we are disgusted; the quarantine between the human and the bestial has been violated. And we see in our reaction the associations between disgust, social convention, dignity, and the sacred. As Douglas notes, "our idea of dirt is compounded of two things, care for hygiene and respect for conventions."[5] The purity violation here, the trigger for the feeling of disgust, is associated with the divinity ethic. Metaphorically, we experience these "uncivilized" acts as a form of desecration, as a form of contamination via a movement away from the angels and toward the animalistic. This is how notions of propriety and dignity become associated with disgust psychology. Failures of dignity and propriety are divinity ethic violations, which are regulated by the compound metaphor of purity and verticality.

3.

But why would any of this create communal conflict? The answer is that, while every society has notions of the sacred, the divinity ethic is a frequent location of social and political dispute. While everyone in a society (generally) recognizes the existence and need for the sacred there is little consensus about what, in our world, requires respect or reverence. There is little consensus about what is or is not "appropriate" or "dignified" in a given situation. Opinions on these matters can vary widely and are hotly disputed. In short, the divinity ethic is deployed unevenly by individuals leading to communal dispute and conflict.

Let me offer a trivial but, I hope, illuminating example of what I'm talking about. I recently delivered a sermon at my church that offended a few people. In the middle of the sermon I read an extended quote from the late David Foster Wallace, sentiments he shared in a commencement address at Kenyon College (and now published in

5. Douglas, *Purity and Danger*, 8.

the book *This Is Water*). After discussing the soul-killing aspects of a typical day in modernity Wallace says this:

> The point is that petty, frustrating crap like this is exactly where the work of choosing comes in.[6]

Wallace goes on to discuss this "work of choosing," the intentional work of finding humanity in the midst of a dehumanizing world. After the sermon I found myself at the center of a congregational kerfuffle. Many congregants were offended that I had used the word "crap" in the pulpit. To many, myself included, this seemed to be a tempest in a teacup, but for others in the congregation a sense of propriety, dignity, and decorum—an attitude commensurate with the sacred space of the sanctuary—had been lost and discarded. My word choice (or, rather, Wallace's) was considered profane and vulgar for a worship service. (I also preached in jeans and with my shirt untucked. These were also considered to be signs of my lack of respect and reverence. In short, my entire persona—my dress and language—was pretty much an offense!)

These are, at root, normative judgments. And they come from the divinity ethic. Something holy and sacred (the worship moment) had been debased by being brought (metaphorically) into contact with something defiling and vulgar ("gutter" language). The elevated tone proper in a worship service had been lost. The emotion this triggers is a sense of revulsion and disgust. The trouble was that this judgment tended to break along generational lines. The older members of the church tended to be the most aggrieved. Most of the younger members of the congregation hardly heard the word "crap" when it was used and, as a consequence, expressed surprise and frustration when informed of the controversy. Younger members of the church couldn't imagine why anyone would get so upset by something so trivial and innocuous. In short, within the congregation we found ourselves in a conflict over the appropriate application of the divinity ethic. What does it mean to be respectful or reverential in our worship moment? Opinions varied wildly on this.

But the problem here is much deeper and more widespread than you might expect. Consider the work of the psychologists Jonathan

---

6. Wallace, *This Is Water*, 76.

Haidt and Jesse Graham concerning the perennial conflicts between liberals and conservatives, in both our churches and within the larger society.[7] Haidt and Graham's research examined how liberals and conservatives differ in how they deploy various moral warrants. Inspired by Shweder's work on moral foundations, Haidt and Graham surveyed anthropological and cross-cultural data comparing and contrasting the various warrants behind normative judgments, the reasons a culture offers for censoring certain behaviors. Why, exactly, is a given behavior prohibited by a community? Why is a certain behavior offensive, taboo, or "wrong"? The warrant behind respect for elders, for example, is likely to be different from the warrants prohibiting theft or murder. The warrant for the former might be an appeal to "hierarchy" (a reference to a status structure governing the life of the community) while the latter might be a straightforward appeal to physical harm or damage. In cataloguing the warrants found in various cultures across the vast terrain of normative judgments, Haidt and Graham expanded upon Shweder's initial list of three (the autonomy, community, and divinity ethics) by identifying five thematic clusters of warrants, what they call the five moral foundations. In short, when a normative judgment is offered in a given culture an appeal is generally made to one of five general warrants. (Simplifying, you might say there are five reasons why anything might be "wrong.")

According to Haidt and Graham the five moral foundations are as follows:

1. *Harm/Care*: Harming others, failures of care/nurturance, or failures of protection are often cited as reasons for an act being "wrong." Some virtues from this domain are kindness, caretaking, and compassion.
2. *Fairness/Reciprocity*: Inequalities or failures to reciprocate are often cited as evidence for something being "wrong." Some virtues here are sharing, egalitarianism, and justice.
3. *Ingroup/Loyalty*: Failure to support, defend, and aid the group is often cited as evidence for "wrongness." Virtues include loyalty, patriotism, and cooperation.

7. Haidt and Graham, "When Morality Opposes Justice," 98–116.

4. *Authority/Respect*: Failure to grant respect to culturally significant groups, institutions, or authority figures is often cause
for sanction. Virtues include respect, duty, and obedience.

5. *Purity/Sanctity*: Anything that demeans, debases, or profanes
human or religious dignity or sacredness is also a cause for
sanction. Virtues include purity, dignity, and holiness.

The foundations of Harm/Care and Fairness/Reciprocity roughly correspond to Shweder's ethic of autonomy. The Ingroup/Loyalty and
Authority/Respect foundations are similar to the community ethic.
The final moral foundation—Purity/Sanctity—corresponds to our
discussion of Shweder's divinity ethic.

The interesting observation made by Haidt and Graham is that
people don't deploy these warrants equally. There are variations between cultures and within a given culture. Take the example mentioned earlier: respect for elders. In a case of generational conflict one
culture or person might defer to the advice, preferences, sensibilities,
or traditions of elders. Such a culture or person defers because the
moral foundation of Authority/Respect is operative in this culture
in regard to elders. But this deference is by no means universal.
Cultures may treat the elderly with greater or lesser respect. And individuals within a given culture might refuse to defer, considering
deference itself to be a bad thing. The point in all this is that different
normative judgments are reached—what is deemed "acceptable" or
"unacceptable"—depending upon which moral foundation is in play
or which foundation trumps in given situation.

Haidt and Graham have observed that this is one of the problems
existing between liberals and conservatives. Specifically, liberals and
conservatives, similar to Jesus and the Pharisees in Matthew 9, differ
in how they deploy and appeal to the five moral foundations. Across
a variety of laboratory tests Haidt and Graham have accumulated evidence that liberals tend to restrict their normative judgment to the
Harm/Care and the Fairness/Reciprocity foundations. That is, liberals
will tend to cry "That's wrong!" when someone is being *harmed/not-
cared-for* or when something is *unfair/unjust*. Liberals don't, as a rule,
often make appeals to the foundations of Ingroup/Loyalty, Authority/
Respect, and Purity/Sanctity. Although liberals are not insensitive or
unmoved by the warrants of Ingroup/Loyalty, Authority/Respect,

and Purity/Sanctity, liberals appeal to these foundations much less frequently when compared to conservatives.

By contrast, conservatives deploy all five foundations when they make normative judgments. This means that a much wider range of stimuli will offend conservatives. Conservatives will be offended by the same stimuli that offend liberals (Harm/Care and Fairness/Reciprocity violations) but will also be offended by stimuli governed by the three other moral foundations (Ingroup/Loyalty, Authority/Respect, Purity/Sanctity). In short, there are many "moral" situations in which liberals will shrug indifferently while conservatives will fume.

As an illustration, consider the status of homosexuality within many churches. When approaching this issue liberals will generally deploy two of the five moral foundations: Harm/Care and Fairness/Reciprocity. That is, liberals will ask "Is anyone being harmed?" and "Is anyone being treated unfairly?" Answering these questions in the negative, liberals will tend to conclude that there is no moral "foundation" (no warrant) for prohibiting homosexuality. If anything, liberals will see civic and ecclesial discrimination toward homosexual persons as the only obvious locations of harm and injustice. This moves the liberal to adopt a permissive stance toward homosexuality. At the very least, it will prompt moral outrage at how churches tend to treat homosexual persons.

Conservatives, by contrast, will consider all five moral foundations and will find amongst the three foundations passed over by liberals warrants for prohibiting homosexuality from the life of the church. Generally, conservatives will make appeals to the foundations of Authority/Respect (e.g., respect for church tradition/teaching) or Purity/Sanctity (e.g., homosexuality is a perversion). Consider how the conservative appeal regarding homosexuality works in light of how we, metaphorically speaking, experience the divinity ethic. By appealing to the Purity/Sanctity foundation conservatives are deploying the compound metaphor of *purity* and *verticality*. By labeling homosexuality a "perversion" conservatives signal both *revulsion* (the disgust response triggered by the purity metaphor) and a movement *downward* on the divinity dimension, a movement away from the sacred toward the bestial and animalistic. Of course, liberals will disagree on this score, rejecting these appeals to the Purity/Sanctity foundation. Liberals would argue that homosexual relations are just as "elevated" and "spiritual" as heterosexual relations.

What all this means is that liberals and conservatives will frequently come into conflict in how they deploy the divinity ethic. And, given that each group is playing by different sets of "rules," each deploying the moral foundations in an idiosyncratic manner, liberals and conservatives will often disagree on normative issues. Unless the conservative agrees to *restrict* her normative judgments to the foundations Harm/Care and Fairness/Reciprocity she will not be able to appreciate the view of the liberal. Conversely, until the liberal agrees to admit warrants from all five moral foundations he will not be able to appreciate the outrage of the conservative.

In sum, liberals will often find appeals to Purity/Sanctity illegitimate (or, more precisely, they will tend to privilege considerations of harm and justice). Conservatives will tend to give these appeals to Purity/Sanctity full consideration and weight and will, frequently, privilege them over appeals to harm and injustice. For example, compare how Jesus and the Pharisees appeal to the various moral foundations in Matthew 9. How do *mercy* and *sacrifice* align with the moral foundations? It seems clear, if we follow the voice of Hosea and the minor prophets, that mercy is aligned with the foundations of Harm/Care and Fairness/Reciprocity. By contrast, sacrifice is clearly an appeal to the foundation of Purity/Sanctity. Given this alignment it can be argued that Jesus is privileging one moral foundation over the other: "I desire mercy, not sacrifice." In light of Haidt and Graham's research, Jesus seems to place himself in the liberal position. No doubt this is exactly how the Pharisees experienced Jesus: as a religious liberal showing disrespect to authority and tradition and flaunting the purity codes by eating with "tax collectors and sinners."

Let me be clear that I'm not co-opting or identifying Jesus with liberal positions in the contemporary "culture wars." The observation that I am making is that "liberalism" is very often, for any given normative issue, the privileging of the foundations of Harm/Care and Fairness/Reciprocity over the foundation of, given our particular focus, Purity/Sanctity. In short, many of the squabbles between liberals and conservatives boil down to the applicability and role of the Purity/Sanctity foundation within the life of the church (and the body politic). Purity, thus, is often a location of communal conflict, with people regularly fighting over divinity ethic violations. When should the divinity ethic be in force? (Can a Christian cuss? Is homosexuality a perversion? Can depictions of the Prophet Muhammad appear in a comic strip?) And when, if ever, should concerns over purity and sanctity be allowed to trump concerns over harm and injustice?

And this situation gets even worse. We've observed how issues of purity and sanctity bring people into conflict. Which wouldn't be so bad if there were ways we could adjudicate between the various appeals to the divinity ethic. Unfortunately, as we will see, appeals to purity and sanctity leave us collectively flummoxed. There appears to be no easy way to resolve these conflicts.

4.

Consider below four "moral situations" from a study conducted by Jonathan Haidt, Silvia Koller, and Maria Dias.[8] As you read each scenario make a normative evaluation: is there anything wrong with this situation?

1. A woman is cleaning out her closet, and she finds her old American flag. She doesn't want the flag anymore, so she cuts it up into pieces and uses the rags to clean her bathroom.

2. A family's dog was killed by a car in front of their house. They had heard that dog meat was delicious, so they cut up the dog's body and cooked it and ate it for dinner.

3. A brother and sister like to kiss each other on the mouth. When nobody is around, they find a secret hiding place and kiss each other on the mouth.

4. A man goes to the supermarket once a week and buys a dead chicken. But before cooking the chicken, he has sexual intercourse with it. Then he thoroughly cooks it and eats it.

In the study the researchers asked participants, as I asked you, if they felt anything was wrong in these scenarios. The answers, as

8. Haidt et al., "Affect, Culture, and Morality," 613–28.

you might expect, were "yes." Participants felt very strongly that a moral principle was being violated in each of these four scenarios. Something was very much amiss.

But in the study the researchers went on to ask the participants to articulate their moral reasoning for making this normative judgment. What moral principle was being violated in each of the scenarios? Interestingly, the participants struggled to produce an answer. As the participants encountered each scenario their normative judgments had a strong, immediate, almost visceral quality. But it was difficult, rationally speaking, to provide clear warrants for those normative feelings and judgments. The participants knew something was wrong, they just couldn't say why.

Jonathan Haidt calls this phenomenon *moral dumbfounding*. Moral dumbfounding occurs when we have a feeling of wrongness but have difficulty articulating coherent moral warrants for those feelings and judgments. The phenomenon of moral dumbfounding is of interest to psychologists because it suggests that in many cases affect is prior to reason when we make normative judgments (as David Hume famously argued). We feel something is wrong and then go in search for rational warrants. And we are often so effective in marshalling these warrants that our success often leads us to think that the warrants created the initial normative judgment, that we encountered a moral situation, reasoned thought it, and then rendered a well-considered, objective moral verdict. We feel that something is wrong because we have made a dispassionate moral calculation. Feeling, in this assessment, follows reason.

The moral dumbfounding research turns this conclusion on its head. By carefully selecting moral scenarios that thwart the rational side of moral judgment, the moral dumbfounding research clearly shows how normative judgments are often *affective* judgments that motivate, in a post hoc fashion, a search for a rational warrant. The warrant in this case is not the decisive factor in reaching the normative judgment. Rather, we seek rational warrants to justify our feelings to others, to give "excuses" as it were, for why we feel the way we do in a particular situation. In this model, then, reason follows emotion. In the language of David Hume, reason is the slave of the passions.

To be clear, there is a continuing debate between the moral traditions associated with Immanuel Kant (reason over passion) and

David Hume (passion over reason) regarding the exact relationship between reason and emotion in normative judgments. But most agree that the moral dumbfounding research demonstrates that emotion is an important and powerful factor in the formation of normative judgments. More, the moral dumbfounding research is important for our purposes as it explains a great deal about communal conflict in evaluating the sacred and holy.

Consider how the moral foundations discussed by Haidt and Graham might apply to the moral dumbfounding scenarios given above. Recall that the moral foundations provide us warrants for making normative judgments. That is, we might examine a moral situation and note that someone was harmed or that some action was unfair. Such judgments are justified by warrants originating from the Harm/Care and Fairness/Reciprocity foundations. But as we read through the moral dumbfounding scenarios above we find that the source of our offense always comes from the Purity/Sanctity foundation. The normative judgment is an appeal to issues of propriety, dignity, and the sacred. These judgments tend to revolve around degradation or a violation of the proper order of things. And it is noteworthy that in many of these dumbfounding scenarios the emotion of disgust is often featured. This is to be expected: we have noted that disgust and the associated feelings of degradation are the affective responses that regulate the Purity/Sanctity foundation.

All this is worrisome as it implies that the experience of the sacred, holy, and divine *is inherently a dumbfounding experience*. This is due to the fact that, as the moral dumfounding research shows, the judgments of Purity/Sanctity are driven by an *emotional* system: specifically, disgust psychology. Given that judgments of Purity/Sanctity are affective rather than rational (the experience of dumbfounding), problems arise in faith communities when there are differences in the felt experiences regarding the divine. That is, what is or is not proper, respectful, or sacred is largely in the eye of the beholder. And given that these are *felt experiences*, rather then rationally derived and publically available arguments, there will be problems in bridging these largely emotional differences.

Consider again the upset in my congregation when I used the word "crap" in my sermon. Recall that people had mixed views on the matter. Some, mainly the older members of the church, saw my word choice as a divinity violation: I was disrespectful. Younger members tended to disagree, feeling that there was nothing offensive or undignified in my language. But the trouble, at this point in the controversy, was that the congregation found itself to be morally dumbfounded. Given that the congregation was working with a Purity/Sanctity violation, offended and unoffended parties had difficulty articulating rational and consensus-building warrants for their respective judgments regarding this situation and what norms should govern future conduct in the pulpit. Imagine one of the younger members trying to find common ground with one of the older members. Why, the younger member might ask, did the older member find the language offensive? The response would likely be (and I know this from experience because I asked these questions) that the language was improper, uncouth, and vulgar. But those aren't warrants. These responses are simply restatements of the normative judgment (i.e., Why did you find the language vulgar? Because it was vulgar.). In a similar way the younger member will have difficultly articulating why a person shouldn't be offended. He or she, personally, didn't feel offended and thus expects that others should feel the same way.

All this is deeply problematic. It means that moral dumbfounding scales up to affect the entire community and complicates how moral and spiritual adjudication is to be accomplished in the church, particularly when notions of the holy and sacred are under consideration (important matters in the church!). Given that Purity/Sanctity judgments are largely affective (rather than rational), groups of people within the church can find themselves with different felt experiences. These differing experiences create conflicting normative judgments about what God may or may not find acceptable or praiseworthy. And, due to moral dumbfounding, little by way of conversation or discussion can rescue the situation. This is the problem noted by Martha Nussbaum in her book *Hiding from Humanity*, where she considers the usefulness of disgust as a warrant in civic discourse. In *Hiding* Nussbaum discusses why disgust, unlike anger, cannot form the basis of law:

Because the notion of harm or damage lies at the core of anger's cognitive content, it is clear that it rests on reasoning that can be publicly articulated and publicly shaped. Damages and harms are a central part of what any public culture, and in any system of law, must deal with; they are therefore a staple of public persuasion and public argument . . . anger (and nonanger) may be misguided, but if all the relevant thoughts stand up to scrutiny, we can expect our friends and fellow citizens to share them and to share our anger . . .

Disgust is very different from anger . . . You can teach a young child to feel disgust at a substance—by strong parental reactions and other forms of psychological influence. Imagine, however, trying to convince someone who is not disgusted by a bat that bats are in fact disgusting. There are no publicly articulable reasons to be given that would make the dialogue a real piece of persuasion. All you could do would be to depict at some length the alleged properties of bats, trying to bring out some connection, some echo with what the interlocutor already finds disgusting: the wet greedy mouth, the rodent-like body. But if the person didn't find those things disgusting, that's that.[9]

A similar analysis holds in the church. Issues of justice and care can be debated, fairly objectively, within the church. We can look at a variety of empirical indicators to see if resources and opportunities are being allocated fairly or if a person is being physically or economically harmed. But if our judgments of the sacred and holy are, at root, felt experiences, then there is little we can point to in the world to build consensus. I simply *feel* offended. That's the beginning and end of my warrant: my subjective experience. So if the felt experiences of the sacred, holy, and divine (and, by definition, the profane, vulgar, and perverse) differ within the church, then groups on different sides of these experiences will be at an impasse, literally dumbfounded by their inability to find common ground. One group finds a behavior offensive, illicit, improper, or perverse. Others don't. And, as Nussbaum notes, very often that's that.

Unfortunately for religious populations, groups deeply committed to the sacred and holy, all this means that large portions of the religious experience will be extraordinarily frustrating, communally

9. Nussbaum, *Hiding*, 99–101.

speaking. Given that the experience of the divine is often regulated by disgust psychology, conversations about God, sin, and holiness are often being torpedoed at some deep level. A dumbfounding is occurring. These dynamics make conversations about God *inherently* difficult because our experience of the divine is being regulated by *emotion* rather than logic, *affect* rather than theology. I think people in churches have always known this, and felt that people in conflict within the church were generally talking past each other. One reason for this is now clear. Very often, arguments and the warrants found within them are *secondary to the felt experience*. Argument is offered to *justify* the felt judgment of the sacred or profane. And as self-justifications these arguments often fail as acts of persuasion or forms of consensus-building.

5.

In the last chapter we surveyed how disgust psychology creates moral problems for individuals. Now, in this chapter, we can see how disgust psychology creates communal problems as well. And there are still other social problems associated with disgust that I'd like to point out here at the end of Part 2 to help transition us to Part 3, the social forms of disgust.

In Chapter 1 we discussed the promiscuity of disgust, how a wide variety of stimuli can elicit disgust reactions. This is often seen in what is called *moralization*, when a previously innocuous behavior begins to be seen in a moral light and to elicit social approbation or disapprobation. For example, you might find smoking to be a "disgusting habit." Thus, when you see someone smoking you can't help but experience slight feelings of disgust, revulsion, contempt, or superiority toward the person who is smoking. Moralization occurs when these feelings of mild disgust or disapproval attach to behaviors or social issues. Notoriously, these feelings wax and wane. What was moralized in one generation is no longer a problem for this generation, and vice versa. Steven Pinker, in his book *The Blank Slate*, offers the following list of things that have become moralized in our generation (with some additions/edits of my own):

advertising to children—automobile safety—Barbie dolls—
"big box" chain stores—big government—cheesecake photos
—clothing from Third World factories—consumer product
safety—corporate-owned farms—defense-funded research—
disposable diapers—disposable packaging—ethnic jokes—
executive salaries—fast food—flirtation in the workplace—
food additives—fur—hydroelectric dams—IQ tests—logging
—mining—nuclear power—oil drilling—owning certain stocks
—poultry farms—public holidays (e.g., MLK day)—research
on stem cells—research on breast cancer—spanking—suburbia
("sprawl")—sugar—tax cuts—toy guns—violence on television
—weight of fashion models[10]

Conversely, there are many behaviors that are becoming amoral-
ized in relation to the feelings of previous generations. As examples,
Pinker lists divorce, illegitimacy, working motherhood, marijuana
use, homosexuality, masturbation, sodomy, oral sex, atheism, and
the practice of non-Western culture.

To be sure, many of the issues listed above involve issues of harm,
danger, and fairness. Many, however, involve emotions of disgust or
revulsion. Consequently, these behaviors become locations of communal dumbfounding as, let's say, the generations differ in how they
feel about certain behaviors. Thus, these behaviors become locations
of communal debate and conflict. Is it appropriate for a Christian to
smoke? Swear? Drink alcohol? Masturbate? If the warrants behind
prohibitive judgments in these cases are based on the Purity/Sanctity
foundation we will tend to end up morally and communally dumbfounded. You feel the behavior is okay. I disagree. And beyond those
felt experiences, what can we say to each other?

But the most worrisome aspect of all this isn't the debate we
are having about what is or is not sacred, holy, dignified, or proper.
It is, rather, how we begin to feel about people engaging in moralized activities. If you moralize smoking (find it disgusting) or swear-
ing (ditto) how do you feel about Christians or non-Christians who
smoke or swear? In short, as we encounter people who participate in
moralized acts (i.e., they engage in activities we disapprove of), it feels
to us that these people move lower on Shweder's divinity dimension.
These people come to represent moral and spiritual contaminants to

10. Pinker, *Blank Slate*, 276.

our collective moral good. If you moralize something like smoking, it is hard to respect smokers. Mild feelings of disgust and contempt begin to emerge. These feelings are focused on both the behavior (e.g., smoking) and on the person engaging in the behavior (i.e., the smoker). Although the behavior itself might not elicit disgust, the person engaging in the behavior is felt to be a fly—a pollutant—in the communal ointment.

This is, perhaps, the most worrisome aspect of disgust. It is not, as we observed in the last chapter, simply that disgust psychology greatly complicates moral reasoning. Nor is it, as we observed in this chapter, that disgust creates problems for communal discernment. No, the real worry concerning disgust is when disgust properties become attached to *people*. As Martha Nussbaum writes:

> If disgust is problematic in principle, we have all the more reason to regard it with suspicion when we observe that it has throughout history been used as a powerful weapon in social efforts to exclude certain groups and persons . . . [disgust] often doesn't stop at feces, cockroaches, and slimy animals. We need a group of humans to bound ourselves against, who will come to exemplify the boundary between the truly human and the basely animal.[11]

What Nussbaum highlights is how, once the divinity dimension is in place, with humans somewhere between the animals and the angels, we begin to rank groups and individuals along this continuum with some groups viewed as higher or superior (e.g., saints) relative to others (e.g., sinners). Inferior groups, those lower on the divinity dimension, therefore begin to take on disgust properties, being closer to the animals than to the angels and superior (truly human) groups.

And this brings us back to the events in Matthew 9. Looking back over Part 2, we analyzed the events in Matthew 9 from a moral perspective. We discussed the Macbeth Effect, the magical thinking involved in contamination appraisals and the entailments of purity metaphors. We also discussed how notions of sin and holiness are regulated by disgust psychology, which creates communal dumbfounding and conflict. And yet all this isn't the most disturbing aspect of Matthew 9. In the end, the real problem in Matthew 9

11. Nussbaum, *Hiding*, 107.

isn't in the *moral reasoning* of the Pharisees, that they shouldn't have framed the situation using a purity metaphor. No, the real problem in Matthew 9 is that the Pharisees saw *human beings as vectors of contamination and pollution*.

We now turn to consider these social aspects of disgust.

PART 3

Hospitality

Do not forget to show hospitality to strangers.

—Hebrews 13:2

5

Love and Boundaries

St. Catherine of Sienna, when she felt revulsion from the wounds
she was tending bitterly reproached herself. Sound hygiene was
incompatible with charity, so she deliberately drank a bowl of puss.

—**Mary Douglas**

1.

You will recall that the adaptive nexus of disgust is called *core disgust*,
the psychology of oral incorporation. More specifically, core disgust
monitors the body envelope protecting us from ingesting contaminated or toxic foodstuffs. But we have also noted that disgust is promiscuous and can attach to many different kinds of stimuli. According
to the system of classification used by Paul Rozin, *sociomoral disgust* is
exhibited when disgust is connected with moral infractions or social
groups. In Part 2 we focused on the moral aspects of sociomoral disgust. Here in Part 3 we turn to the social manifestations of disgust.

As noted in Chapter 1, the modern study of disgust began with
Charles Darwin. In his book *The Expression of Emotions in Man and
Animals* Darwin gave us, perhaps unwittingly, a classic example of
sociomoral disgust. Specifically, recall Darwin's story about the "savage" he encountered on his HMS *Beagle* trip:

> In Tierra del Fuego a native touched with his finger some cold
> preserved meat which I was eating at our bivouac, and plainly

73

showed disgust at its softness; whilst I felt utter disgust at my
food being touched by a naked savage, though his hands did
not appear dirty.[1]

Both core and sociomoral disgust intermingle in this narrative.
Core disgust is plainly seen in how both Darwin and the native center their disgust on food. However, sociomoral disgust is evidenced
in Darwin's disgust at a "naked savage" touching his food. That is,
in sociomoral disgust people and entire populations can be seen as
sources of contamination. Thus, contact with these persons can elicit
the strong revulsion of the disgust response. Note that the divinity ethic is also implicated (in which humans are seen as "between"
angels and animals on a vertical dimension). The person touching
Darwin's meat is "naked" and a "savage." Although Darwin was fairly
enlightened for his day when it came to race (abolitionism ran deep
and hot in his family), we get the sense from Darwin that the British
gentleman is higher up the scale of human cultural evolution: closer,
presumably, to the divine and further, presumably, from the beasts.
Darwin's focus on nudity is diagnostic. There is something base and
undignified about the lack of clothing. It is animalistic. Once again
we see disgust mingle with notions of the divine and profane.

Sociomoral disgust can extend, on a case-by-case basis, to individuals we deem "disgusting," "revolting," or "creepy." We make
these attributions for a variety of reasons (e.g., poor hygiene, moral
failures). Regardless as to the source of the attribution, we experience
feelings of revulsion in proximity to these people.

Further, sociomoral disgust can apply to entire populations.
Racists tend to view the despised group as a source of contamination. This happened in America with the slave population and in
Nazi Germany with the Jewish population. But these are hardly the
only examples. Wherever hate, racism, or genocidal impulses exist,
sociomoral contamination and disgust take center stage. As the philosopher Martha Nussbaum observes:

> Throughout history, certain disgust properties—sliminess, bad
> smell, stickiness, decay, foulness—have repeatedly and monot-
> onously been associated with, indeed projected onto, groups

---

1. Darwin, *Expressions*, 256.

by reference to whom privileged groups seek to define their superior human status.[2]

This picture is even more troubling when we remember that religious systems often institutionalize, overtly or tacitly, sociomoral disgust. The most obvious example of this is the Hindu caste system in which people are born into the "Untouchable" caste of society. But Hinduism is by no means atypical in this regard. In the Old Testament, the people of Israel viewed the surrounding tribes as sources of potential defilement. In Christianity, distinctions are made between the church and "the world" with the encouragement, according to James 1:27, to "keep oneself from being polluted by the world."

Sociomoral disgust sits at the heart of the conflict in Matthew 9. The problem was that a class of people—"tax collectors and sinners"— were understood to be, intrinsically, a form of pollution. Strongly, these people were *waste*, contaminants, vectors of contagion. Thus, contact with these persons was prohibited if one wanted to maintain a stance of holiness and purity.

And Matthew 9 is by no means the only example of this in the gospels. Jesus routinely moves into the domain of sociomoral disgust. Consider two other examples, the first from Luke 7:

> Now one of the Pharisees invited Jesus to have dinner with him, so he went to the Pharisee's house and reclined at the table. When a woman who had lived a sinful life in that town learned that Jesus was eating at the Pharisee's house, she brought an alabaster jar of perfume, and as she stood behind him at his feet weeping, she began to wet his feet with her tears. Then she wiped them with her hair, kissed them and poured perfume on them.
>
> When the Pharisee who had invited him saw this, he said to himself, "If this man were a prophet, he would know who is touching him and what kind of woman she is—that she is a sinner."

Again, the issue here is a worry over *contact*. The complaint is, specifically, about the person "who is touching him" combined with "the kind of woman she is."

Another example comes from Matthew 8:

2. Nussbaum, *Hiding*, 107–8.

> When he came down from the mountainside, large crowds fol-
> lowed him. A man with leprosy came and knelt before him
> and said, "Lord, if you are willing, you can make me clean."
> Jesus reached out his hand and touched the man. "I am will-
> ing," he said. "Be clean!"

What is intriguing about this story is the sequence. Jesus touches
the leper first. Then the command "Be clean!" is offered. That is,
Jesus' first move is *into ritual defilement*. By first touching the leper,
Jesus intentionally and willfully *seeks* contamination, standing in
solidarity with the unclean. This is striking because the expected
sequence would be initial purification followed by contact. Jesus,
surprisingly for the onlookers, does the opposite. Contact occurs
first. Purification follows solidarity. And one can only wonder how
various Christian communities approach this sequence in their own
missional endeavors.

What is curious in the New Testament is that, despite the example of Jesus in the gospels, sociomoral disgust continued to plague
and hamper the early church. Specifically, in the book of Acts we are
told the early church was failing to take the message of Jesus "into
the world." In the early chapters of Acts the church was still orbit-
ing the Temple and its cleansing rituals. The gospel was making few,
if any, inroads into the Gentile world. And the reason for this was
sociomoral disgust.

We know this to be the case because of the events recounted in
Acts 10. It is clear in Acts 10 that the gospel message was not making
its way into the larger Gentile world because uncircumcised Gentiles
were regarded as a source of sociomoral contamination. Given this
crisis God moves decisively in Acts 10, arranging a meeting between
Peter, the Jew, and Cornelius, the Gentile. In a vision to Peter, God
dismantles Peter's sociomoral disgust psychology. Peter is in prayer
upon a housetop. While in prayer a vision of "unclean" animals in a
sheet is lowered from heaven. A voice prompts Peter to rise, kill, and
then eat the animals. Given that the purity tradition of Leviticus has
declared these animals to be "unclean" and not fit for consumption,
Peter rejects the offer of food, stating that he should not eat anything "unclean." The voice from heaven then retorts, "Do not call
anything impure that God has made clean." This sequence happens

three times. After the final sequence, Cornelius' messengers arrive and Peter, deeply puzzled, accompanies them to Cornelius' house. At the house, after Peter and Cornelius exchange stories recounting their visions, Peter proceeds to proclaim the good news of Jesus.

Peter's vision of unclean animals is an excellent illustration of the psychology of disgust and nicely illustrates how core and sociomoral disgust fuse and mix, just as we saw in Darwin's story. When asked to eat the "unclean" animals, core disgust is the presenting problem for Peter. That is, issues of food and food-aversions are being discussed. But the issue, Peter eventually discovers, is not about contaminated *food*, it's about contaminated *people*. Core disgust is the surface level problem, but sociomoral disgust is the deeper issue. What is striking about this story, in light of the empirical work on disgust, is how psychologically sophisticated it is, how disgust is being uprooted at its psychological base. In Peter's vision God dismantles the contamination boundary between Jew and Gentile so that the gospel message could break forth into the entire world.

2.

In short, sociomoral disgust is deeply woven into the fabric of the biblical narrative. And what we see in texts such as Matthew 9 and Acts 10 is ambivalence about the existence of sociomoral disgust in the life of Israel and the early church. However, to fully appreciate this ambivalence it might be helpful to place the events in Matthew 9 within a larger narrative context. This will help illuminate the stakes in Matthew 9 concerning the conflict between mercy and sacrifice. Specifically, one way to approach the events in Matthew 9 is to see how Jesus, in light of this reading, was rethinking notions of holiness and righteousness in the life of Israel. As we have observed, notions of holiness demand quarantine, boundaries between the sacred and profane. In the life of Israel these boundaries functioned, as they often do, as forms of social control and exclusion. In light of Haidt and Graham's research we could say that Israel was privileging the moral foundation of Purity/Sanctity. This privileging, however, created certain noxious social outcomes that offended the moral foundations of

Harm/Care and Fairness/Reciprocity. And many in Israel were find-ing this righteousness-through-exclusion to be morally problematic. As Miroslav Volf observes in his book *Exclusion and Embrace*:

> An advantage of conceiving sin as the practice of exclusion is that it names as sin what often passes as virtue, aseptically in religious circles. In the Palestine of Jesus' day, "sinners" were not simply "the wicked" who were therefore religiously bank-rupt, but also social outcasts, people who practiced despised trades, Gentiles and Samaritans, those who failed to keep the Law as interpreted by a particular sect. A "righteous" person had to separate herself from the latter; their presence defiled because they were defiled. Jesus' table fellowship with "tax col-lectors and sinners," a fellowship that indisputably belonged to the central features of his ministry, offset this conception of sin. Since he who was innocent, sinless, and fully within God's camp transgressed social boundaries that excluded outcasts, these boundaries themselves were evil, sinful, and outside God's will. By embracing the "outcast," Jesus understood the "sinfulness" of the persons and systems that cast them out.[3]

As Volf notes, in the gospels Jesus reframes notions of sinfulness. Rather than focusing on "unclean" *people* Jesus focuses on the *bound-ary* separating "clean" from "unclean." As Volf says, "these boundar-ies themselves were evil." The inherent difficulty with this reframing was that Jesus' notion of sin—exclusion—brought him into conflict with the Levitical purity codes (or how those codes were interpreted). Holiness demands boundaries and quarantine. Jesus' ministry of table fellowship was dismantling these boundaries and breaking the quarantine.

But what Jesus was doing was not wholly unanticipated. The purity tradition had been problematized by Israel's prophets in their concern that the priestly tradition of holiness, sacrifice, and purity was, in some fundamental way, missing the point. According to the prophets, God demands justice over purity, mercy over sacrifice:

> I hate, I despise your religious feasts; I cannot stand your as-semblies. Even though you bring me burnt offerings and grain offerings, I will not accept them. Though you bring choice fel-lowship offerings, I will have no regard for them. Away with

---

3. Volf, *Exclusion and Embrace*, 72.

the noise of your songs! I will not listen to the music of your harps. But let justice roll on like a river, righteousness like a never-failing stream! (Amos 5:21–24)

For I desire mercy, not sacrifice, and acknowledgment of God rather than burnt offerings. (Hosea 6:6)

In short, there was a dissonant chord in the life of Israel regarding the purity trajectory, a tension between the prophetic and priestly traditions. As Walter Brueggemann summarizes:

[The purity and justice] trajectories of command serve very different sensibilities *and live in profound tension with each other.* The tradition of justice concerns the political-economic life of the community and urges drastic transformative and rehabilitative activity. The tradition of holiness focuses on the cultic life of the community and seeks a restoration of a lost holiness, whereby the presence of God can again be counted on and enjoyed.[4]

I have been suggesting that the "profound tension" between mercy and sacrifice wasn't a historical accident. Rather, mercy and sacrifice are *intrinsically* incompatible, due largely to psychological factors we will illuminate shortly. But the upshot of this incompatibility was that there needed to be some way to resolve the tension, to adjudicate between the prophetic and priestly traditions in the life of Israel.

As we see in texts like Matthew 9, this tension spilled forward into the New Testament. Which tradition—priestly or prophetic—should guide the life of Israel? And to be clear, this is no false dichotomy. The issue isn't logical. It is, rather, a conflict, a fundamental disjoint, between the lived experiences governed by either the priestly or prophetic impulses. When it comes to moral discernment the two impulses, in a fairly lawful fashion, point in opposite directions. And Israel, individually and collectively, had to choose which way to go.

Thus, one way of approaching the gospel accounts is to see Jesus formally addressing the unresolved conflict between the purity and justice traditions within the life of Israel. One example of this reading is Fernando Belo's *A Materialist Reading of the Gospel of Mark.* According to Belo, the tensions in the gospel of Mark are between

4. Brueggemann, *Theology of the Old Testament,* 192. Italics are mine.

systems he calls *contagion/pollution* and *debt*. These correspond to the priestly and prophetic traditions, the tension between sacrifice and mercy. As Jesus enters the world of Mark he finds Israel dominated by two competing conceptions of "sin." The first is the purity tradition, what Belo describes as the contagion view of sin:

> In Israel, then, as in other human societies, the symbolic system is organized first and foremost as a defense against the violence of contagion, the impurity of the confused and formless . . . The rational organization of productive work and everyday life therefore requires taboos relating to pollution and warding off the threatened danger which pollution represents. The focal points of the symbolic systems are centers of purity from which is excluded the impure, the misshapen, the undifferentiated, anything that breaks down forms . . . Pollution means confusion and the dissolution of the elements involved; it is a *curse*. People reject it to the point of avoiding even simple contact or *touching*, since the impure is so violent as to be contagious.[5]

These "centers of purity" were, as Belo describes, "centers of consumption":

> In Israel the symbolic field was organized around three centers, each of which corresponds to one of the three instances of social formation. All three were centers or foci of consumption: the *table*, the *"house"* (in the sense of a group of kinspeople; that is what the quotation marks around the word indicate), and the *sanctuary*; this means the consumption of food at meals, consumption of bodies in sexual activity, and ideological consumption in religious sacrifice.[6]

Once again we see the intermingling of core (food consumption) and sociomoral (social exclusion) disgust, where food aversions are generalized to sociomoral spaces such as table-fellowship, familial affection, and religious participation. Consequently, certain persons, based upon appraisals of contagion, were excluded from these sociomoral spaces: table, house, and sanctuary. These "unclean" people were denied table-fellowship and access to sacred spaces. Into this milieu Jesus enters, preaching a subversive message that undermines

5. Belo, *Materialist Reading*, 38–39. Italics in original.
6. Ibid., 38.

the contagion view of sin by allowing the "unclean" entrance into the "family space" of table fellowship.

Similar to Volf's analysis above, Belo argues that Jesus inverts the contagion view of sin by viewing table fellowship through the lens of the justice tradition. Belo calls this tradition *debt* and defines its moral failures as forms of *violence*. Belo argues, as we have been arguing, that the systems of contagion and debt were fighting for the hearts and minds of Israel. Contagion separated the pure from the contaminated by drawing a boundary around the pure and relegating the unclean to the "outside." And if one transgressed the sociomoral barriers (even in the name of love) the purity codes would have been violated. The two systems were at an impasse.

To break the impasse, Belo argues, the writer of Mark sets out to show that Jesus has the power and authority to overturn and rein-terpret the purity tradition. For example, in the first chapter of Mark Jesus triumphs over the contagion system on two occasions. First, in verse 23 a man with an "unclean" spirit is found in a sociomoral space, the synagogue. Jesus heals this man. Later, in verse 40, Jesus encounters a man with leprosy. The leper asks to be made "clean." Jesus touches the man and responds, "Be clean!" As we have already observed, in this healing Jesus reverses the directionality and power of pollution (the attribution of negativity dominance). Rather than the unclean polluting the clean, we see, in Jesus' touch, the clean making the polluted pure. Here, in Jesus, we see a reversal, a *positive contamination*. Contact *cleanses* rather than pollutes. In short, in these two early episodes in Mark we see a demonstration of Jesus' power over the contagion system.

Soon after these events, in a parallel to Matthew 9, Jesus is found admitting "unclean" persons—tax collectors and sinners—to the sociomoral space of table-fellowship. This trajectory of events reaches a culmination in Mark 7 where Jesus and the Pharisees explicitly debate issues of purity and contamination. The issue, again, is a conflation of food (core disgust) and holiness (sociomoral disgust): eating with "unclean" hands. Jesus declares that what makes a person "unclean" is what flows out of the heart of the person and has nothing to do with what they eat. The sins that Jesus lists as "pollutants" of the heart, Belo situates squarely within the debt system of sin:

[It] is the heart (inside) and the evil machinations (outside), [which are] the things that really pollute humanity. The list of the evils belongs to the debt system (theft, murder, adultery, and avarice; the others are variants that can be easily inscribed in these four), a fact already indicated by the seat assigned to them, namely, the heart. The key to the opposition of the two circuits in which the components are not directly equivalent (foods and evil machinations) is to be found in the inside/outside scheme. The inside is the stomach in one case, the heart in the other. What comes from the stomach goes into the privy (a place of pollution and filth); what comes from the heart are practices involving debt (aggression).[7]

Volf joins Belo at this point:

Central to . . . strategies for fighting exclusion is the belief that the source of evil does not lie outside of a person, in impure things, but inside a person, in the impure heart (Mark 7:15). [Thus,] the pursuit of false purity emerges as a central aspect of sin—the enforced purity of a person or a community that set itself apart from the defiled world in a hypocritical sinlessness and excludes the boundary breaking other from its heart and its world. Sin is here the kind of purity that wants the world cleansed of the other rather then the heart cleansed of the evil that drives people out by calling those who are clean "unclean" and refusing to help make clean those who are unclean. Put more formally, sin is "the will to purity" turned away from the "spiritual" life of the self to the cultural world of the other . . .[8]

In all of this, Jesus is seen as deconstructing the purity tradition. Jesus redefines purity as failures of mercy, as failures of the heart. Jesus wants to remove notions of "purity" from the social sphere to, in effect, eliminate sociomoral disgust from the life of Israel. For mercy is impossible when sociomoral disgust is operative.

A stronger formulation of this conclusion is to say that Jesus is privileging the prophetic tradition over the priestly tradition. In the great debate between the two traditions, Jesus resolves the "profound tension" by decisively siding with the prophetic impulse. Jesus explicitly echoes the prophets and declares that God desires "mercy, not sacrifice."

7. Ibid., 143–44.

8. Volf, *Exclusion and Embrace*, 74.

3.

But why do we have to choose? Why not honor both traditions? Why is mercy seen as trumping sacrifice?

We've traced the conflict between the two impulses through the Old Testament and into the gospel accounts. And I've repeatedly said that this conflict is not historical or accidental, that there is a lawful relationship between mercy and sacrifice that reliably and inexorably brings them into conflict. It's now time to examine the relationship between mercy and sacrifice.

As mentioned above, it will be important to illuminate this dynamic because critics might object that the tensions here are illusory and manufactured, a false dichotomy that is easy to resolve. Logically, perhaps, this might be true. There seems to be no reason to assume that mercy and sacrifice might not have significant intersections, areas of overlapping concern. The game doesn't have to be zerosum. But I think such criticisms fail on two accounts. First, such criticisms fail to appreciate the very real conflict between the priestly and prophetic traditions in the life of Israel. The conflict between these traditions was not the result of the rabbis being poor logicians, that they failed to see the very obvious false dichotomy sitting smack in the middle of their religious life. We can assume the rabbis could have cleared up any logical errors fairly quickly and easily. No, the tensions between the priestly and prophetic traditions were not logical or set-theoretic. The solution wasn't a simple switch from "either/or" to "both/and." Further, such a solution misses the breathtaking teaching of Jesus. Jesus doesn't need to be so radical. He could have simply said: God desires mercy *and* sacrifice. Instead, Jesus echoes Hosea's more radical claim: God desires mercy, *not* sacrifice. Phrased another way, given how Jesus deconstructs sacrifice in the gospels, God demands mercy *as* sacrifice.

The second problem with logical objections is that they fail to understand that life under the priestly and prophetic impulses creates different lived experiences. Different metaphors of righteousness are deployed, generating different emotions, entailments, and psychological responses, both individually and communally. Parts 1 and 2 of this book were devoted to describing life under the purity

*Is this anti-Jewish
well known — priest
prophets*

impulse. In short, the Pharisees were not making a logical error in Matthew 9. They were living within a coherent moral and social paradigm. Unfortunately, that paradigm was producing noxious social and moral outcomes. Consequently, this purity paradigm had to be jettisoned: not for any logical problem, but due to the fact that the holiness impulse reliably produces such immoral outcomes. Further, any logical or theological objections fail to realize how sacrifice continues to impede mercy in the life of the church. As churches explore missional living, they routinely come into conflict over the tensions inherent in mercy and sacrifice. Churches have to make choices, often walking what seems to be a razor edge, trying to balance the imperatives of holy living and missional engagement. Again, as every church leader knows, this isn't a logical confusion. Holding mercy and sacrifice together is difficult and treacherous. Very often, because we loathe cognitive dissonance, and from the sheer fatigue of discernment, churches tend to resolve the tension by breaking one way or the other, falling toward either mercy or sacrifice. Turning outward or turning inward.

In short, the conflict between mercy and sacrifice is not a logical error. Something more is going on. Specifically, there is a *psychological* conflict between mercy and sacrifice. What makes the tension so real and acute is that mercy and sacrifice create lived experiences that are fundamentally incompatible. Consequently, to achieve coherence we must, in a very real way, "choose" between the two impulses. I've made this claim repeatedly throughout these chapters. It's now time to illuminate the machinery, the dynamic at the heart of this tension.

4.

As I said in the Introduction, my first glimmer of understanding about the dynamics at work in Matthew 9 occurred when I encountered Paul Rozin's Dixie cup experiments. These simple experiments dramatically illustrate the boundary-monitoring functions of disgust. As Martha Nussbaum describes:

> Disgust concerns the borders of the body: it focuses on the prospect that a problematic substance may be incorporated

into the self . . . The disgusting has to be seen as alien: one's own bodily products are not viewed as disgusting so long as they are inside one's own body, although they become disgusting after they leave it. Most people are disgusted by drinking from a glass into which they themselves have spat, although they are not sensitive to the saliva in their own mouths.[9]

Obviously, few people find swallowing their own saliva disgusting. But disgust emerges when the saliva is expelled and we are asked to reincorporate it into the body. The distinction here, as Nussbaum observes, pivots off of notions of interiority and exteriority. The saliva in my mouth is *inside*, it is a part of me. Thus, I feel no disgust in swallowing. By contrast, the saliva I expel from my body is now, suddenly, on the *outside*, not a part of me.

It is, perhaps, no exaggeration to suggest that the Dixie cup demonstration illustrates, both psychologically and metaphorically, the core dynamic of sociomoral disgust. The self is defined by a boundary. That which is inside this boundary is embraced as a part of the self. That which is outside of this boundary is rejected as alien and other. And this distinction is emotionally marked by the disgust response.

Of course, the Dixie cup example focuses on core disgust, revulsion centered on the act of oral incorporation. In core disgust the boundary being monitored is the body envelope and its orifices. In core disgust "selfhood" is defined at the edge of the body.

But humans are symbolic creatures, and "selfhood" extends well past the edges of the body. Selfhood is a symbolic identification that reaches into the world to "own" and identify with people, places, objects, events, communities, and ideas. Marriage provides an example of this extension and fusion. In the language of Genesis two people become "one flesh." The boundary of the self is symbolically extended to include the partner. Ernest Becker has a wonderful description of this extended, symbolic self:

The body is *one* of the things in which our true feelings are located, but it is not the only one, and it may not even be the principal one . . . Least of all is the self limited to the body. A person literally projects or throws himself out of the body, and

9. Nussbaum, *Hiding*, 88.

anywhere at all. As the great William James put it almost 80 years ago: A man's "Me" is the sum total of all that he can call his, not only his body and his mind, but his clothes and house, his wife and children, his ancestors and friends, his reputation and works, his lands and horses, his yacht and his bank-account. In other words, the human animal can be symbolically located wherever he feels a part of him really exists or belongs . . . You get a good feeling for what the self "looks like" in its extensions if you imagine the person to be a cylinder with a hollow inside, in which is lodged his self. Out of this cylinder the self overflows and extends into the surroundings, as a kind of huge amoeba, pushing its pseudopods to a wife, a car, a flag, a crushed flower in a secret book. The picture you get is of a huge invisible amoeba spread out over the landscape, with boundaries very far from its own center or home base.[10]

The image of the self extended and spread over the world like a huge amoeba is striking and apt. Cognitively, this extended self is represented as a set enclosed by a border. The world is thus divided into the "Me" and the "Not-Me." Selfhood is, at root, a boundary. It may be a fuzzy and porous boundary, but a boundary nonetheless.

As the self gets symbolically extended so does disgust psychology, the primal psychology that monitors the boundary of the body. Disgust accompanies the self as it reaches into the world, continuing to provide emotional markers denoting "inside" versus "outside," the boundary points of the extended symbolic self.

With this understanding of the self in hand, we are well positioned to understand human love, intimacy, and relationality. Specifically, as the notion of "one flesh" highlights, love is a form of inclusion. The boundary of the self is extended to include the other. The very word intimacy conjures the sense of a small, shared space. We also describe relationships in terms of proximity and distance. Those we love are "close" to us. When love cools we grow "distant." We tell "inside" jokes that speak of shared experiences. We have a "circle of friends." "Outsiders" are told to "stop butting in." We ask people to "give us space" when we want to "pull back" from a relationship. In sum, love is inherently experienced as a boundary issue. Love is on the *inside* of the symbolic self.

10. Becker, *Birth and Death of Meaning*, 33–34.

Given that disgust monitors the boundaries of selfhood and intimacy it should come as no surprise then that love involves a suspension of disgust and contamination sensitivity. More strongly, disgust is a *prerequisite* of love. Love, to be love, requires a backdrop of disgust. For someone to move "inside" there must be a pre-existing condition of having been "outside," being exterior and other. In short, disgust establishes boundaries of contact. Love enters as a secondary mechanism when those boundaries are transgressed or dismantled. As William Miller, in his excellent book, *The Anatomy of Disgust*, describes:

> One way of describing intimacy (and/or love) is as that state in which various disgust rules are relaxed or suspended . . . Changing diapers, overcoming the disgust inherent in contaminating substances, is emblematic of the unconditional quality of nurturing parental love. Without such overcoming, the act would have no emblematic significance. Love means a kind of self-overcoming in this context, the overcoming of powerful aversions, and the suspension of purity rules that hold you in their grip. It means that your fastidiousness, your own purity of being, must be subordinated to the well-being of the next generation.[11]

This dynamic is clearly illustrated in the case of human sexuality. As Miller notes, sexual love and pleasure are only possible when pre-existing disgust rules are suspended:

> A person's tongue in your mouth could be experienced as a pleasure or as the most repulsive and nauseating intrusion depending on the state of relations that exist or are being negotiated between you and the person. But someone else's tongue in your mouth can be a sign of intimacy because it can also be a disgusting assault. The marks of intimacy depend upon the violability of Goffman's "territories of the self." Without such territory over which you vigilantly patrol the borders there can be nothing special in allowing or gaining access to it . . . Consensual sex means the mutual transgression of the disgust-defending boundaries.[12]

11. Miller, *Anatomy of Disgust*, 133–34.
12. Ibid., 137.

In the symbolic, emotional, and physical aspects of sex we see how disgust regulates the boundaries of selfhood. Love and intimacy involves the dismantling of these boundaries of the self. For example, early on in romantic love we grant access to our personal and symbolic space through *permission*, like accepting that tentative request for a first kiss. Eventually, as love progresses, this boundary-transgression is less a matter of permission and more one of psychic fusing. As Miller summarizes:

> One might hazard the idea that in their early stages relations of intimacy and love seem more governed by the regime of rights and grants, but with the passage of time and the routinization of permitted boundary transgressions, the loved one passes eventually from an intimate autonomous other to something more akin to one's own vital organ . . . . So in the end two fleshes are made one.[13]

What we discover in all this is that disgust and love are *reciprocal processes*. Disgust *erects* boundaries while love *dismantles* boundaries. This was the conclusion of St. Catherine noted in the quote at the start of the chapter: sound hygiene was incompatible with charity. One also thinks of St. Francis rushing up to kiss the leper. Love is, at root, the suspension of disgust, the psychic fusion of selves.

5.

It should now be clear why there is a "profound tension" between mercy and sacrifice. What we have discovered is that mercy and sacrifice are not two distinct moral logics. Rather, mercy and sacrifice are manifestations of a single, unified moral faculty. Miroslav Volf has called this logic *exclusion and embrace*. Obviously, given Volf's terms, it is impossible to exclude and embrace at the same time. Psychologically speaking, we now understand how this works. Embrace, as a manifestation of love, involves boundary transgression. Exclusion, by contrast, erects sociomoral boundaries. Unfortunately, as we have discussed, notions of purity and holiness require sociomoral boundaries to be erected. Holiness and purity are expulsive practices. Consequently, it

13. Ibid., 141–42.

is difficult to reconcile notions of holiness and purity with acts of solidarity, embrace, and inclusion. At critical moral junctures, one must choose: exclusion or embrace? In Matthew 9, for example, Jesus selects embrace while the Pharisees select exclusion.

In one sense, this analysis is not new and simply revisits other more exhaustive theological and moral analyses (e.g., Volf's treatment in *Exclusion and Embrace* and Jürgen Moltmann's in *The Crucified God*). What is novel in this psychological approach is how it illuminates the experiential tensions inherent in making missional choices. More, it demonstrates how these tensions are both ubiquitous and difficult to avoid. By activating notions of purity, holiness, and sanctity *along with* notions of mercy, love, and hospitality, the church activates a host of metaphors, images, and psychological impulses that are, experientially speaking, conflicting, contradictory, and confusing. Again, this conflict isn't logical. This is an experiential conflict, a disjoint within the lived experience. In short, calls for embrace, hospitality, or solidarity will flounder if churches are not attentive to the psychological dynamics governing these experiences. Calls for love and community are all well and good, but churches often undermine these efforts by failing to help their members understand and navigate their psychological experiences of purity and holiness. Purity *via inclusion*, the notion guiding Jesus in Matthew 9, is counterintuitive and, thus, fragile. It's simply not natural to think this way. Calls for embrace are swimming upstream against an innate and ingrained psychology.

Further, if exclusion and embrace inherently involve an either/or dynamic, due to the psychological mechanics involved, then calls for hospitality are greatly complicated. Bland "both/and" recommendations tend to fail because they underestimate the reciprocal nature of love and disgust. This is the reason that bromides like "love the sinner but hate the sin" are often so ineffective. Empathy and moral outrage, for reasons we have been discussing, tend to function at cross purposes. These psychological responses tend to be reciprocally related—more of one means less of the other.

Given the either/or nature of the psychology involved, we face thorny discernment issues. Specifically, will the call for inclusion and embrace destroy the moral and spiritual integrity of the faith community? Transgressing boundaries is integral to the act of embrace. But in this embrace will distinctiveness and integrity be lost? If all sociomoral boundaries are dismantled, the church will lose its peculiar life and character. At some point, it seems, the church will have to erect a purity boundary to define and protect its shared life and defining commitments. We'll revisit these issues in Chapter 8. For now, however, we have come to understand how the conflict in Matthew 9 was not accidental or situational. Mercy and sacrifice reliably come into conflict due to the reciprocal nature of love and disgust, the psychological dynamics governing exclusion and embrace. Consequently, the church cannot sidestep the tensions in Matthew 9 as a mere logical error or false dichotomy. Whenever the church speaks of love or holiness, the psychology of disgust is present and operative, often affecting the experience of the church in ways that lead to befuddlement, conflict, and missional failure.

6

Monsters and Scapegoats

From the time (perhaps around age seven or eight) when children
somehow learn to play with those ubiquitous paper devices
known as "cootie-catchers," pretending to catch foul bugs from
the skin of children who are disliked or viewed as an out-group,
children practice a form of disgust-based social subordination
known to all societies, creating groups of humans who allegedly
bear the disgust-properties of foulness, smelliness, contamination.

—Martha Nussbaum

1.

In the last chapter we introduced the dynamics of sociomoral disgust and discussed the psychological tensions inherent in notions
of mercy and sacrifice, the reciprocal nature of disgust and love. In
this chapter and the next we will continue to examine the effects
of sociomoral disgust in the life of the church. We will start in this
chapter by examining extreme forms of sociomoral disgust, exclusion at its genocidal worst. This analysis might not seem relevant for
good-hearted people. However, sociomoral disgust is often the engine
of social scapegoating, religiously and politically. True, on a day-to-
day basis few of us struggle with sociomoral disgust, the province of
hate-mongers and racists. But during times of social stress and crisis,
sociomoral disgust can infect a population. Consequently, churches

need to be prepared for these eventualities as religious institutions often legitimize and sanction witch-hunts and scapegoating (be it religious, social, or political). In addition, sociomoral disgust doesn't emerge out of nowhere. As Nussbaum notes in the quote above, this dynamic—attributing disgust properties to people—emerges early in human development and is used to identify the weak and subordinate, producing prejudice, persecution, ostracization, and exclusion. Even the best of us, as we'll see, struggle with sociomoral disgust.

2.

Sociomoral disgust can vary in severity. On the playground, "cooties" seems harmless and innocuous (unless you've been on the other end of that game). But sociomoral disgust can quickly scale up in intensity and become the engine behind the very worst of human atrocities. During times of social stress or chaos, those persons or populations already associated with disgust properties will provide the community a location of blame, fear, and paranoia. In short, sociomoral disgust is implicated in the creation of *monsters* and *scapegoats*, where outgroup members are demonized and selected for exclusion or elimination. As David Gilmore writes in his book *Monsters*, a monster is "the demonization of the 'Other' in the image of the monster as a political device for scapegoating those whom the rules of society deem impure or unworthy—the transgressors and deviants." These deviants are considered to be "deformed, amoral, [and] unsocialized to the point of inhumanness."[1] Take, for an example, the Nazi propaganda film *The Eternal Jew*, where an early shot in the film showed rats emerging from a sewer juxtaposed with a crowd of Jewish persons in a Polish city. In America, as another example, proponents of anti-gay legislation have circulated pamphlets claiming that gay men eat human feces and drink human blood. In each of these instances, sociomoral disgust is used to demonize and scapegoat populations, creating "monsters" who are threatening to society.

The "monster" tends to be the nadir of sociomoral disgust, the final outworking of its logic in which people are dehumanized to

1. Gilmore, *Monsters*, 14.

the point of being ontologically Other. Worse, monsters are sub-human *and* malevolent, a source of social threat and danger. This is important to note as the category of "monster" tends to mask the mechanisms of social scapegoating. Scapegoating has become, for the most part, morally transparent. When named, we consider scapegoating to be a social evil. In contrast, the monstrous tends to obscure the scapegoating mechanism. It does this in two ways. First, the monstrous activates disgust psychology. And once activated these feelings of revulsion justify the acts of social exclusion or violence. Second, while scapegoats are considered to be innocent and passive, monsters are dangerous, malevolent, and threatening. Again, this threat justifies violence against the "monster." In short, the category "monster" is a visceral and emotional category that fuels the acts of social scapegoating. By analyzing the monstrous in relation to the scapegoat, we are able to focus upon the social psychology of groups where the real moral battle against scapegoating is to be waged. No one knowingly engages in scapegoating. But crusades against monsters are all too common.

The word "monster" has its origins in the Latin *monstrum* meaning "omen" or "warning." Given this meaning we might ask, what are monsters warning us about? A start on an answer comes from the anthropological literature. David Gilmore notes that monsters are cultural universals. Every culture has its monsters. And across cultures monsters appear to share similar characteristics. Gilmore lists many of these:

- Aggressive
- Gigantic
- Man-eating
- Malevolent
- Hybrids
- Gruesome
- Atavistic
- Powerful
- Violent[2]

2. Ibid., ix.

Fear dominates this list. Fears of predation. Fears of destruction. But, as noted above, disgust also seems implicated in the monster schema. Monsters, visually and in their behavior, trigger revulsion and disgust. From Gilmore's list I'd like to analyze how purity and disgust are implicated in the feature of hybridization.

Monsters are often ontological mixtures, blends, and composites. A quick tour through the world of mythology and legend shows us this: minotaurs, centaurs, fauns, mermaids, Pegasus, unicorns. But many of these hybrids are not very monstrous. They are strange, otherworldly, and uncanny. But unicorns and centaurs don't seem to be monsters, widely understood. In short, monsters are not simply hybrids. They are a certain *kind* of hybrid. If so, what kind?

Generally speaking, the hybrid must be transgressive, illicit, and taboo. The question then becomes, what makes a mixture illicit? Why am I not repulsed by angels (i.e., the depiction of winged people) but find a man with a bug-head monstrous?

I believe the illicit mixing seen in monsters is the same mixing we considered in Chapter 4. Recall how disgust regulates the divinity dimension, monitoring the mixing of the holy and the profane. Given that sociomoral disgust is implicated in the creation of monsters (e.g., stigmatized groups like the Jews in Nazi Germany) it should come as no surprise that monsters are *divinity violations*. Something "high" on the divinity dimension is being mixed with something "low." A man with a bug-head is taboo as it mixes something sacred (the human person created in the *Imago Dei)* and brings it into contact with something low and base, in this example an insect. By contrast, in Western traditions wings are symbols of the heavenly and the angelic. Thus, when wings are seen in depictions of angels we find the human/wing hybrid elevating rather than monstrous. In the propaganda art of Nazi Germany the Jew was hybridized with rodents. This rat/human hybrid allowed the Nazis to create a monster out of the Jew and, as a consequence, create widespread sociomoral disgust within the German population.

In short, the monster is often a symbol of degradation and contamination. In this, the monster is *sub*-human, another example of the divine/vertical metaphor we discussed at length in Part 2. This degradation triggers disgust and activates the expulsive response.

The monster must be expelled or eliminated. This means that, once created, the monster often functions as a scapegoat. Again, this was clearly illustrated in Nazi Germany. Not only were the Jews made out to be monsters, they were also blamed and scapegoated for the German defeat in WWI and the nation's subsequent humiliation.

As noted earlier, the "logic" of the scapegoat works if the scapegoat is seen as an object of defilement. This attribution activates disgust psychology which, in turn, makes scapegoating seem reasonable, intuitive, and right. Somehow, purification is accomplished by an act of *expulsion*. Something vile on the "inside" is forced "out." Scapegoating is the religious and social analogue of the vomit response in disgust, a violent rejection of a contaminant from the body. This is the same dynamic seen with the expulsion of monsters from the community. Monsters and their ilk, representing degradation and defilement, must be expelled from the community to secure a "cleansing." Thus, it is no coincidence that the rodent-like Jew (the monstrous hybrid) fit nicely with the Nazi notion of national, blood, and ethnic purity, an association that created what Daniel Goldhagen has called the *eliminationist* anti-Semitism of the Final Solution. Anti-Semitism was common in Europe but the rise of the peculiar *exterminative* facet of Nazi thinking appeared to be fueled by the prominent role that *purity* played in the Nazi's racial and political ideology. In all of this we see how disgust, purity, and eliminationist impulses are implicated in the creation of social monsters as objects of scapegoating and ethnic "cleansing."

3.

The great moral temptation in scapegoating is that it often feels justified and righteous. The sinful mechanism is often hidden from view. Witch-hunts tend to be fueled by religious and moral fury. In fact, there is a very intimate connection between scapegoating and the experience of the sacred. And, due to this close association, religion is often at the forefront of social scapegoating.

As many know, the great expositor of the links between society, religion, and scapegoating is Renè Girard. In his book *Violence and the*

Sacred, Girard describes how scapegoating was transformed into religious sacrifice in primitive cultures and, as a consequence, became a powerful tool of social cohesion. Specifically, scapegoating occurs when the community is undergoing stress (e.g., famine, epidemic, war). During these times of fear, people grow anxious, distrustful, and paranoid. And this fear propagates through the community until the entire group is facing massive outbreaks of violence. At this juncture, one of two things will occur. If the group doesn't find a way to vent its paranoia and aggression, violence breaks out and, given the imitative facet of human nature, will escalate in reciprocal bouts of revenge killing. Eventually, due to the unchecked violence, the society will disintegrate.

But Girard suggests that, at the height of communal violence, many cultures took an alternative route, a tragic but effective route. For some reason, different at different times and places, the ire of the group fell upon a certain person or subgroup. A scapegoat for the collective misfortune was identified. And in that moment of identification, group solidarity miraculously reappears. Once-fractured individuals now stand together against the scapegoat. The violence of the group is brought to bear upon the One to save the Many, and the sacrifice occurs. And in the wake of the sacrifice the blood lust of the now-unified group is sated. Peace returns.

This is the theory of the origin of primitive religion offered by Girard in *Violence and the Sacred*. Girard contends that scapegoating sacrifice emerged in human history as the solution to a very real problem: the management of communal violence. Human societies are volatile (due to fact that humans compete for the same goods, opportunities, and resources, what Girard calls mimetic rivalry): ready, at a moment's notice, to burst into violence. Sacrifice was the cultural innovation that aided humans in managing this violence. Moreover, the scapegoat unites the once-divided group. With the sacrifice of the scapegoat, a violent mob is both pacified and united. This communal catharsis appears "magical" and, according to Girard, became associated with supernatural power and significance. Over time the scapegoat and the sacrifice became incorporated into the mythic structures of the group's metaphysical worldview. The sacrifice becomes necessary, eternal, and sanctioned by the gods.

Scapegoating, according to Girard, was the engine behind primitive sacrifice-based religion, those religions' experience of the sacred. The theologian S. Mark Heim in his book *Saved from Sacrifice* nicely summarizes the scapegoating mechanism and its subsequent association with the sacred:

> The sad good in this bad thing is that [scapegoating] actually works. In the train of the murder [of the scapegoat] the community finds that this sudden war of all against one delivers it from the war of each against all. The sacrifice of one person as a scapegoat discharges the pending acts of retribution between members of the group. It "clears the air." The contagion of reciprocal violence is suspended, a circuit breaker has been thrown. The collective violence is reconciling because it reestablishes peace. This benefit seems a startling, even magical result, an outcome much greater than could be expected from a simple mob execution . . . The one mobbed as the most reprehensible criminal now is revered as the bringer of peace, one with a divine vocation to die and restore order for the people. So the victim becomes a god, memorialized in myth, and the killing becomes a feature of a foreordained plan, a pattern and a model. In the face of future threats, similar response will be required. Rituals of sacrifice originated in this way, tools to fend off social crisis. And in varied forms they are with us still.[3]

In all of this we see connections between *purity* and *violence*, further illuminating why Jesus, in Matthew 9, privileges mercy over the sacrificial impulse, an impulse driven by the social scapegoating inherent in Israel's notions of purity and holiness. Further, it is also no coincidence in Matthew 9 that Jesus' acts of table fellowship created an experience of the monstrous, a transgressive union of the sacred and the profane. And, as an experience of the monstrous, Jesus' actions were perceived as malevolent and dangerous. Later in the gospels Jesus is eventually identified with the devil and, in light of this attribution, becomes a religiously sanctioned object of scapegoating sacrifice.

As noted above, the creation of the monstrous tends to obscure the psychology behind scapegoating practices. Again, scapegoating has become (and Girard would claim that the gospel accounts were critical in this regard) a fairly transparent process, morally speaking.

3. Heim, *Saved from Sacrifice*, 43–44.

When exposed, we understand scapegoating to be a social evil. But the category of the monster is less transparent, and yet, as we have seen, it follows the same pattern of Girardian scapegoating. We don't think we are scapegoating when we go after monsters because, well, they are *monsters*. For example, although we can see the scapegoating inherent in Nazi anti-Semitism, the category of "monster" (the transgressive hybrid of the rat-like Jew) obscured the mechanism from the conscience of Germany. The Final Solution was perceived as "righteous" because monsters were going to the gas chambers, not scapegoats.

Our analysis of the monstrous in sociomoral disgust supplements the Girardian literature regarding the association between scapegoating and the sacred. This supplement helps illuminate how the scapegoat is selected in the first place. Specifically, sociomoral disgust is often a key factor. Recall Nussbaum's description of the social dynamics of the playground. From childhood, humans are adept in sorting people according to purported disgust properties. The odd, lonely, and weak on the playground become the "smelly," the "creepy," and the "disgusting." Consequently, these children are singled out for peer violence. These kids, selected by sociomoral disgust, become the scapegoats and, via the Girardian mechanism, unite their peers by focusing and channeling their violence. In a similar way, sociomoral disgust guides the selection of scapegoats at the communal level during times of social crisis and stress.

Of course, the scapegoats are often innocent. As Girard argues in his book *Things Hidden Since the Foundation of the World*, Jesus unmasks the scapegoating mechanism by being declared "innocent" (in the eyes of the gospel reader) while the characters in the story scapegoat Jesus as "guilty." We are aware, as we read the gospels, that a peace has been achieved, but it is a peace predicated upon killing. We observe how the sacrifice of Jesus does its job by restoring a real, if tenuous, peace between the mob and the religious and political authorities during the socially volatile Passover celebrations in Jerusalem. The gospels do tell us that the key religious and political players—Herod and Pilate—became *friends* in the aftermath of Jesus' death. As Heim noted, the sacrifice "worked": it restored the "peace." But for readers of the gospel, the violent mechanism of this "peace" is exposed and discredited. The "peace" of sacrifice is no peace at all. We know the scapegoat was innocent.

But did not Jesus he became
God wanted him to do
this.

So we moderns, in the wake of the gospel, have grown wary of scapegoating. We know "witch hunts" are often misguided and immoral. And this observation also converges upon the monster myths. Monsters are, strangely, both victims *and* victimizers. This imbues monster stories with a complicated ambivalence. At the communal level monsters are malevolent and dangerous. This provokes the expulsive response. But many monster stories, like the gospel accounts, have a subplot that sits in tension with the dominant expulsive narrative. Often, the monster is discovered to be kind, charitable, and human. The violent mob, in fact, is now the true monster. In a Girardian inversion we come to identify with the monster over those who seek to kill him. The stories of Frankenstein and Disney's *Beauty and the Beast* come to mind. Embedded in the monster myth is the gospel-induced fear that we, in seeking to kill monsters, have become the monster. It is as Nietzsche warned in *Beyond Good and Evil*: "Whoever fights monsters should see to it that in the process he does not become a monster."

4.

The "monster" is sociomoral disgust at its most severe, and it illustrates, in the extreme, the associations between purity/sacrifice and expulsive violence. These associations are important to note due to the fact that, while scapegoating has become more transparent, the monstrous has not. This is largely a consequence of the fact that the monstrous is an attribution fueled by the passions, very often the emotions of disgust and revulsion. Monsters are transgressive hybrids, objects of desecration and degradation. Consequently, sociomoral disgust makes it difficult for us to step back from monster-hunting crusades to expose the scapegoating mechanisms at work within our own hearts and minds.

But these examples are extreme. Yes, of course, sociomoral disgust is observed in racism, anti-Semitism, virulent homophobia, and genocide, but few of us feel like we participate in or are vulnerable to these social evils. Realistically speaking, how often do we feel emotions of disgust around people?

Although we all can think of "disgusting" people we might know, our general assessment is that sociomoral disgust isn't a regular feature in our workaday lives. But such a conclusion is worrisome in that extreme forms of social exclusion don't spring out of nowhere. As we noted earlier, sociomoral disgust emerges on the playground and, as we'll see, never really leaves us. Small sociomoral fissures run through our hearts and minds, fissures that can be exploited if we are not vigilant. Few of us actively go looking for scapegoats or monsters, but we can get pulled into these activities if we are not careful.

How, then, might sociomoral disgust be affecting us in ways outside of our awareness? Let's begin to answer that question by considering some features of human moral psychology. Specifically, the ethicist Peter Singer in his book *The Expanding Circle* has described the human moral faculty as a simple two-stage process. The first process is a classification mechanism that differentiates "kin" or "family" from "non-kin." We see this instinct emerge with the onset of stranger anxiety in young children. Young babies don't show anxiety around strangers. A baby can be passed around among friends, family, and strangers without the child minding very much. But toddlers, after the onset of stranger anxiety, are much more reticent at being left with or held by strangers. And with the onset of stranger anxiety we see the human person begin to carve the world into two groups: family versus strangers.

Once we identify our "family" the second mechanism of the moral instinct emerges. It follows a simple rule: extend "kindness" toward our "kin." That is, familial affection is instinctively extended to members of our "tribe." As we know, "kindness" and "kin" share the same semantic root. We extend "kindness" to those of the same "kind." Altruism follows our ontology.

These two instinctive processes create what Singer calls our *moral circle*. That is, we psychologically draw a circle around a group of people whom we identify as "my kind," "my tribe," "my clan," "my family." This circle is initially populated with family members, but as we grow the circle includes more and more non-biological relations, "friends" who are "like family to us." Once you are admitted into this moral space, affection and warmth flow naturally and instinctively. I don't have to work at feeling affection for my wife, mother, sons, or best friends. Inside the moral circle affection is like breathing; it's just a natural part of being human. This is largely due to the mechanisms observed in the last chapter, the psychic fusion and identification of the extended symbolic self. Otherness is lost when you are "inside" the moral circle.

But what about those people on the outside of the moral circle? Those we identify as strangers? People on the outside of the moral circle are treated *instrumentally*, as tools to accomplish our goals in the world. In Kantian language, people inside the moral circle are treated as *ends* in themselves while people on the outside of the moral circle are treated as *means* to our ends. We treat those inside the moral circle with love, affection, and mercy, and those outside the moral circle with indifference, hostility, or pragmatism. And all this flows naturally from a simple psychological mechanism: Are you identified as "family"? Once the identification is made (or not), life inside and outside the circle flows easily and reflexively.

I use the following scenario in my classes to illustrate the nature of the moral circle. Imagine, I ask my students, that your best friend just got a job waiting tables at a restaurant. To celebrate with her you arrange with friends to go to the restaurant to eat dinner on her first night. You ask to be seated in her section and look forward to surprising her and, later, leaving her a big tip. Soon your friend arrives at your table, sweating and stressed out. She is having a terrible night. Things are going badly and she is behind getting food and drinks out. So, I ask my students, what do you do? Easily and naturally the students respond, "We'd say, 'Don't worry about us. Take care of everyone else first.'" I point out to the students that this response is no great moral struggle. It's a simple and easy response. Like breathing. It is just natural to extend grace to a suffering friend. Why? Because she is inside our moral circle.

But imagine, I continue with the students, that you go out to eat tonight with some friends. And your server, whom you vaguely notice seems stressed out, performs poorly. You don't get good service. What do you do in that situation? Well, since this stranger is not a part of our moral circle, we get frustrated and angry. The server is a tool and she is not performing properly. She is inconveniencing us. So, we complain to the manager and refuse to tip. In the end, we fail to treat another human being with mercy and dignity. Why? Because in a deep psychological sense, this server wasn't really "human" to us. She was a part of the "backdrop" of our lives, part of the teeming anonymous masses toward which I feel indifference, fear, or frustration. The server is on the "outside" of my moral circle.

Now you might be wondering, am I being too harsh? Is this server really seen as "not fully human"? The answer might surprise you. The anthropologist Levi-Strauss once wrote that "Humankind ceases at the border of the tribe."[4] We've already seen, given Singer's notion of the moral circle, that how we treat people depends upon whether they are a part of my "tribe." But Levi-Strauss' comment is stronger. Does *humanity* end at the edge of the moral circle? That is, is the way we treat people outside the moral circle symptomatic of something darker and more sinister? Do we see outsiders as less than human?

The phenomenon of seeing people as less than human is called infrahumanization.[5] Historically, infrahumanization occurs when one group of people comes to believe that another group of people does not possess some vital and defining human quality such as intellect or certain moral sensibilities. These infrahumans might be human from a biological perspective, but they are believed to lack some moral or psychological attribute that makes them fully human, on par with the "superior" group. And as we have seen, sociomoral disgust is critically involved in the process of infrahumanization. For example, in America a classic case of infrahumanization is found in the first U.S. Constitution (Article 1. Section 2) in which slaves were considered, for the purposes of the census, to be three fifths of a person. And, in psychological support of this state-sanctioned infrahumanization, disgust properties were attributed to the slaves: bad smell, filthiness, animal-like features, imbecility. The two processes, disgust and infrahumanization, often go hand in hand.

But again, this seems like an example of extreme behavior. Does it apply to everyday relationships? Yes it does. Specifically, social psychologists studying the mental dynamics of group psychology have shown infrahumanization to be an inherent feature of how we reason about group membership. This is largely due to the fact that humans

4. Levi-Strauss, *Race and History*, 21.
5. Demoulin et al., "Infrahumanization," 153–71.

tend to reason about categories in terms of *essences*. That is, when we make distinctions of kind we tend to think that some essential property distinguishes the two groups being classified.[6] For example, when we contrast humans with animals we tend to not see the difference as one of *degree*. Rather, we speculate that some intrinsic and essential property is possessed by humans that is lacking in animals (e.g., humans have souls and animals do not). Obviously, education and critical thinking can override these essentialist accounts. But essentialist reasoning seems to be our natural, unconscious, and default way of thinking about group membership. It is a mode of thinking that emerges in childhood and persists throughout the lifespan.

In short, when we think about groups—white vs. black, gay vs. straight, Christian vs. Muslim, rich vs. the poor—our natural instinct is to find some essential property that separates the groups, a quality that one group has that the other lacks. For example, one often hears in discussions about the welfare state that the poor might lack the "discipline" or "moral character" that characterizes productive citizens. We can see in this how essentialist reasoning is shaping how group differences are understood, and not helpfully so.

Infrahumanization occurs, then, when we, as a member of a group, begin to apply essentialist reasoning to out-group members. More specifically, my "tribe" is considered to be the ideal, the standard of being fully human. Thus, almost by definition, the out-group must lack some quality that marks the fully human standard. This denial of a defining human characteristic begins the process of infrahumanization. But the important thing to note is how infrahumanization occurs *naturally* as we reason about group membership. Infrahumanization isn't just the extreme behavior of racists. Our essentialist mode of thinking makes it an everyday affair.

Take, for example, the work of the psychologist Jacques-Philippe Leyens.[7] Across a variety of studies Leyens and colleagues observed how normal persons, like you and me, make associations regarding people perceived to be in my "tribe" (which can be defined by race, gender, or any other grouping characteristic) versus those perceived

6. Leyens et al., "Psychological Essentialism," 395–411
7. Demoulin et al., "Infrahumanization," 153–71.

to be outside my "tribe." The question was, does humanity, as Levi-Strauss suggested, end at the edge of the tribe?

Again, infrahumanization occurs when we begin to deny some essential human characteristic to an out-group member. Often, this characteristic is intelligence or some other moral or emotional quality. Leyens has focused on the attribution of primary and secondary emotions to in-group and out-group members. To understand this, we need to stop for a moment and talk about emotions.

Primary emotions are considered to be common across animal species, mammals in particular. Primary emotions include pain, pleasure, fear, joy, surprise, and anger. Primary emotions are not uniquely human. For instance, a dog as well as a human can experience pain, fear, or joy. Secondary emotions are subtler shades of emotions. They are often blends of the more basic primary emotions. Examples of secondary emotions include love, hope, admiration, pride, conceit, nostalgia, remorse, and rancor. Compared with the primary emotions the secondary emotions are quintessentially human: they are intuitively felt to be more cognitive, moral, internally caused, and mature. These are the higher, more exquisite emotions. Summarizing the distinction, Leyens suggests a simple test to determine if an emotion is primary or secondary: "Would I apply this emotional term to an animal such as a rabbit or a fish?" We expect that we could surprise a fish or that a rabbit might be fearful. Consequently, these are examples of primary emotions. But we don't tend to think of fish as being prideful or nostalgic. These are the secondary emotions, the emotions that separate humans from animals.

Returning now to infrahumanization: given the animal/human distinction between primary and secondary emotions, one symptom of infrahumanization would be denying secondary emotions to out-group members. Consider again the example of slavery in the American South. Slaveholders had no hesitance in attributing primary emotions to the slaves. Like any animal, slaves could be happy, afraid, or angry. But slaveholders hesitated in attributing secondary emotions to the slaves. Again, these are the emotions that are quintessentially human. Consequently, if a slave woman was separated from her children at auction, could she really feel that separation as acutely as a white mother could? The answer, unsurprisingly, was no, she could not. The slave woman was not fully human. She lacked secondary emotions.

Again, it might seem that judgments such as these are extreme, but across multiple studies, many conducted by Leyens, it has been demonstrated that while we easily attribute both primary and secondary emotions to in-group members (my "tribe") we are much more reticent about attributing secondary emotions to out-group members. These effects are subtle, but they can be measured in reaction-time tests (i.e., how quickly you attribute an emotion to an in-group and out-group target). These effects have been shown to apply to race, nationality, and even to people who work in your office (in-group) or not (out-group). We are members of many kinds of "tribes" and we, due to essentialist reasoning, tend to see those on the "inside" as more human than those on the outside.

But should we be concerned about infrahumanization measured in millisecond differentials in reaction-time tests? I believe we should. Psychologists have long known that these slight biases and associations often have measurable behavioral effects. Effects we are often unaware of. For example, as we interview people for jobs we are very often unaware of how the applicant's skin color, gender, weight, or accent is affecting us. We feel our final hiring choice is objective and impartial. And yet, churning beneath the surface are biases and prejudices that are affecting our decisions. Biases we never notice or evaluate.

As mentioned earlier, racism and hate just don't emerge out of the blue. The research concerning infrahumanization suggests that fissures run through every human heart. In good times and with good people these fissures might not amount to much. But the effects are scalable and can add up. When we aggregate the effects we see discrimination in hiring practices, pay differences, social exclusion, and votes to deny marginalized groups access to basic freedoms. These macro-level forms of exclusion are difficult to trace back to single individual actions. The effects of infrahumanization are only noticeable when the micro-level decisions are examined in aggregate and across time.

In addition, these in-group/out-group fissures within our hearts provide the dry kindling for the Girardian scapegoating mechanism. In times of plenty and peace we don't feel the need to locate a scapegoat. The fissures within our hearts remain small. But during times of stress and panic these fissures begin to crack open. And the search for a scapegoat commences. Consider, for example, how Americans treated citizens of Japanese descent after the bombing of Pearl Harbor. Or how American Muslims are regarded in the wake of 9/11. Ponder how Americans have become more tolerant of torture.

What is intriguing about the infrahumanization research is that it brings us back to monsters. Recall, monsters are often sub-human. Monsters are lower on the divinity dimension, more bestial than human. This is, at root, what is happening in infrahumanization, pushing out-group members away from the human toward the animal. The difference between "monsters" and infrahumans is only a matter of degree. And the truly scary part of this dynamic is that it is a regular feature of how we reason about social life. In sum, the dynamics of sociomoral disgust apply to us all, everyday. Sociomoral disgust isn't limited to cases of homophobia, racism, or genocide. As we noted at the start of the chapter, the social dynamics of sociomoral disgust—scapegoating, exclusion, and violence—emerge on the playground and we never fully escape them. True, the intensity of the social exclusion may vary. And the degree of infrahumanization may vary from milliseconds in labs to the gas chambers at Auschwitz. But the fissures exist in every human heart.

7

Contempt and Heresy

You did not treat me with contempt or scorn. Instead, you welcomed
me as if I were an angel of God, as if I were Christ Jesus himself.

—**Galatians 4:14**

In this chapter I want to continue to explore everyday experiences
with sociomoral disgust by examining a closely related emotion—
contempt. An exploration of contempt will prove fruitful for three
reasons. First, we will observe how contempt, in a manner similar
to disgust, functions as a boundary psychology. These observations
will reinforce and complement our analysis in Chapter 5 regarding
the reciprocal nature of disgust and love. Second, while sociomoral
disgust may be a relatively rare experience for many of us, the emotions of disdain, superiority, and contempt are fairly common. Who
can avoid feeling smug around certain sorts of people? Thus, the con-
tempt/disgust link will allow us to extend our analysis even deeper
into everyday existence. And I am very keen to get this point across.
My fear is, given the strength of the disgust response, that people
will conclude that sociomoral disgust is symptomatic only of very
extreme behavior, the purview of racists and bigots. But as I tried
to show toward the end of the last chapter (and hope to show in
this one), the dynamics of disgust are everyday affairs. Finally, our
focus on contempt will allow us to examine another failure of table

fellowship in the New Testament. Specifically, we will trace the emotions of disgust and contempt through the book of 1 Corinthians, observing how these emotions were creating social fractures within the Corinthian church. Surprisingly, these fractures were manifesting themselves in the very ritual—the Lord's Supper—that functioned as a reenactment of Jesus' ministry of table fellowship.

1.

It was Darwin, not surprisingly, who first described the close association between disgust and contempt. In Chapter 11 of *Expressions of the Emotions in Man and Animals*, Darwin discusses the associations between disgust, contempt, and disdain. Darwin notes that contempt and disgust share common facial expressions, most notably the wrinkling of the nose. Darwin writes:

> The most common method of expressing contempt is by movements about the nose, or round the mouth; but the latter movements, when strongly pronounced, indicate disgust. The nose may be slightly turned up, which apparently follows from the turning up of the upper lip; or the movement may be abbreviated into the mere wrinkling of the nose . . . We seem thus to say to the despised person that he smells offensively, in nearly the same manner as we express to him by half-closing our eyelids, or turning away our faces, that he is not worth looking at.[1]

We described the facial expression of disgust in Chapter 1. Contempt shares many of these same features. Contempt is the proverbial "turning up one's nose." It is the scornful sneer and the aristocratic sniff of disdain. These are the same facial expressions we observe in disgust, expressions associated with an oral rejection response. And Darwin notes an additional association between disgust and contempt, also involved with oral rejection—the act of spitting:

> Spitting seems an almost universal sign of contempt or disgust; and spitting obviously represents the rejection of anything offensive from the mouth. Shakespeare makes the Duke

---

1. Darwin, *Expressions*, 255–56.

of Norfolk say, "I spit at him—call him a slanderous coward and a villain."[2]

Darwin concludes that both disgust and contempt serve the same expulsive and boundary-monitoring function:

> We have now seen that scorn, disdain, contempt, and disgust are expressed in many different ways, by movements of the features, and by various gestures; and that these are the same throughout the world. They all consist of actions representing the rejection or exclusion of some real object which we dislike or abhor . . .[3]

Contempt is generally distinguished from disgust in that it introduces a hierarchical component. Not only do we wrinkle our noses in contempt, we "look down our nose" at the people offending us. That contempt is a hierarchical emotion shouldn't be surprising. Recall that disgust regulates the divinity ethic, which is metaphorically understood to be a vertical—"higher" versus "lower"—dimension. What is lower and closer to the animals is "looked down on" from the more elevated human perspective. Thus, it is no surprise that "superior" groups experience both disgust and contempt in response to "inferior" groups.

The close association between disgust and contempt is also seen in our analysis of love and intimacy. Recall, disgust defines the boundaries of selfhood and otherness. The act of love, for example when two fleshes become "one" (psychically or physically), is experienced as a boundary transgression in which the other is granted access to the "interior" of my life. If this analysis is accurate, then it stands to reason that when the intimacy erodes we should see a reemergence of disgust and contempt. That is, as loved ones drift apart, emotionally speaking, they should begin to reexperience sociomoral distance and separation. In the marital relationship "one flesh" begins to separate back into two. Otherness reemerges, marked by the onset of disgust. The once intimate and erotic touch of the spouse is now experienced as an intrusion, a violation. Physical intimacies such as sex are no longer relished but experienced as disgusting and revolting. With the

2. Ibid., 261.
3. Ibid., 262.

collapse of love disgust reemerges to erect and monitor a boundary between the self and the other.

This analysis is no idle or theoretical speculation. Consider the research of John Gottman, the premier researcher regarding the dynamics of marriage and divorce. Specifically, Gottman and his colleagues have shown that future divorce can be reliably predicted by watching newlyweds interact as they discuss an emotionally charged issue.[4] In these studies Gottman and colleagues have newlywed couples discuss an aspect of their marriage that is a point of conflict. During the interaction the researchers code the emotions of the husband and wife as they discuss the conflict. Gottman's research has shown that divorce can be successfully predicted for newlywed couples if negative emotions dominate over positive emotions in the exchange. Importantly for our purposes, the negative emotions that most strongly predict subsequent divorce are the emotions of contempt and disgust.

This result might be surprising to some. We might have guessed that anger would be more diagnostic of marital distress. However, having learned a bit about disgust and otherness, we know that Gottman's findings are exactly what we would expect from the dissolution of love and intimacy. Given that both contempt and disgust are implicated in hierarchy (feelings of superiority) and infrahumanization (judgments that a person is sub-human), it should be clear how disgust and contempt would signal the severest kind of relational distress. No doubt anger is problematic in relationships, but anger is not hierarchal nor is it inherently dehumanizing. But feeling superior towards one's spouse or feeling disgusted by a spouse are clear signs of relational distress. The emergence of disgust and contempt signal that "one flesh" has separated into otherness. The sociomoral barriers that were once blurred or non-existent have, sadly, snapped back into place. What was once embraced as an object of love has dissolved back into the alien and exterior.

This examination of marriage is important because it demonstrates, once again, how disgust and contempt monitor the boundaries of intimacy and otherness in everyday interactions. Although we might not experience strong revulsion around people, most of us

4. Carrère and Gottman, "Predicting Divorce," 293–301.

struggle with experiences of contempt, scorn, or disdain for others. And as we see in marriages, these feelings signal the failure of intimacy and inclusion. Further, Gottman's marriage research continues to illustrate the reciprocal nature of love and disgust inherent in the way these emotions erect (exclusion) or dissolve (embrace) relational boundaries. Each signals the dissolution of the other.

2.

Revisiting Matthew 9, it seems clear that contempt was implicated in the attitudes of the Pharisees. We can imagine the expressions of disdain on the faces of those criticizing Jesus' association with unsavory people. Jesus' ministry of table fellowship challenged these judgments of superiority by proclaiming a radical egalitarianism within the Kingdom of God. In this, Jesus' ministry not only dismantled barriers of sociomoral disgust (by removing the distinctions between the clean and unclean) but also challenged the social hierarchies and power structures that fuel the emotion of contempt.

The early church was also characterized by this radical egalitarianism and embrace of otherness. However, this was a fragile business, with notable failures documented in the New Testament. Peter, the first to cross the sociomoral boundary between Jew and Gentile in Acts 10, struggles to maintain this embrace. According to Paul's account in Galatians 2, in the face of social pressure Peter is tempted to "separate" from the Gentile believers, refusing to engage with them in table fellowship. In short, despite the example of Jesus the practice of table fellowship was a location of conflict and struggle within the early church (yet another example of how core and sociomoral disgust are frequently conflated). Ingrained psychological and behavioral habits made table fellowship socially volatile. We can imagine how hard it would have been for new Christian converts to switch off or repress deeply ingrained feelings of contempt and sociomoral disgust when they were asked to participate in the egalitarian hospitality of Christian worship and fellowship. Occasionally, as with Peter, sociomoral barriers would reemerge and fracture the fellowship. And similar to a struggling marriage, the reemergence of sociomoral barriers within the fellowship (e.g., Jew vs. Gentile, high status vs. low status) would be signaled by the presence of disgust and contempt within the community of believers. The experiences within the church at Corinth will provide us with an excellent case study of this dynamic.

From a psychological perspective, the case of Corinth is illustrative because the emotional dynamics of exclusion—contempt and disgust—are clearly on display. More, because the issues in Corinth were socioeconomic in nature rather than disputes over Levitical purity codes, the troubles in Corinth are more accessible to modern readers. The events in Matthew 9 might seem alien and strange to many of us. Few of us divide our social worlds into the "clean" and "unclean." But all of us can identify with the social tensions inherent in issues of hierarchy, status, and socioeconomic class. We routinely experience how these socioeconomic forces motivate acts of exclusion. In short, although modern readers might not fully appreciate the purity violations involved in Matthew 9, most of us continue to struggle mightily with the transgressive nature of Jesus' egalitarianism. And the emotion of contempt, as we will see in Corinth, features prominently in these struggles.

3.

Many of the problems in Corinth were on display during their times of table fellowship, the communal meal that was associated with the celebration of the Lord's Supper. That sociomoral barriers were being erected during the Lord's Supper was particularly disturbing to Paul, and we can understand his anger. Given that the Lord's Supper symbolized and reenacted Jesus' ministry of table fellowship, entering into his practices of welcome, inclusion, and hospitality, it was outrageous that the Lord's Supper had became a location of exclusion and social stratification. This unholy inversion of the egalitarian nature of the ritual was symptomatic of a profound moral and social failure within the Corinthian church. That the Lord's Supper had become an instrument of exclusion was a sign that something had gone terribly wrong.

The fact that the Corinthians' failure in their celebration of the Lord's Supper was a moral and communal failure is highlighted if we approach the Lord's Supper from a social psychological perspective, for it is striking that the central act of Christian worship is metaphorically understood to be a family meal around a table. Kinship language is extended to non-relatives, where the "brothers" and "sisters" in Christ share a "supper" as members of God's "family." The Lord's Supper universalizes the language of family and kinship. People dislocated by race, blood ties, and socioeconomic class are embraced and included through their participation in the Lord's Supper. Consequently, this ritual dramatically symbolizes and reenacts (in flesh and blood) the ministry of Jesus in the gospels. More, the practice of the Lord's Supper prepares the Christian community for *mission*. After practicing welcoming others (and being welcomed in return) to the "Lord's Table" Christians leave the ritual to practice embrace *at every table*. As Samuel Wells writes in his book *Improvisation: The Drama of Christian Ethics*:

> By sharing bread with one another around the Lord's Table, Christians learn to live in peace with those with whom they share other tables—breakfast, shop-floor, office, checkout. They develop the skills of distribution, of the poor sharing their bread with the rich, and the rich with the poor. They develop the skills of equality, of the valued place of the differently abled, differently gendered and oriented people, those of assorted races and classes and medical, criminal and social histories.[5]

Psychologically, we observe in all this how the practice of the Lord's Supper expands the moral circle. By universalizing kinship language the Lord's Supper is actively pushing against the sociomoral fissures of disgust and contempt. The Lord's Supper, through its metaphors and the missional practices it promotes, is a ritual that is fundamentally altering and remaking the psyche. The Lord's Supper reconfigures the way we experience otherness. More specifically, the Lord's Supper is a practice that dismantles the psychic fissures within the heart that create otherness. Inherent in the ritual is boundary transgression, the movement we observed in intimacy and love. This boundary transgression creates contact between the "clean" and the

5. Wells, *Improvisation*, 83.

"unclean" as seen in Matthew 9 or Acts 10, signaling the elimination of disgust and the associated purity entailments from the life of the community. The boundary transgression also involves contact between the "high" and the "low," a stratification often driven by socioeconomic distinctions, eliminating the emotions of contempt, pride, and superiority from the life of the church.

What this analysis reveals is that the Lord's Supper is a profoundly deep and powerful psychological *intervention*. At the basement level, where the seeds of exclusion are sown, the symbols and practices of the Lord's Supper restructure our experiences of otherness. Through imagination and participation, the psychology of disgust, which activates the dynamics of exteriority and exclusion (from simple disdain to genocide), is dismantled and rebuilt into the image of Christ.

Participation in the Lord's Supper, then, is an inherently *moral* act. In the first century church, and in our own time, people who would never have associated with each other in the larger society sit as equals around the Table of the Lord. I am reminded of these lines by Walt Whitman in *Leaves of Grass*:

> This is the meal pleasantly set . . . this is the meal and drink
> for natural hunger,
>> It is for the wicked just the same as for the righteous . . . I
> make appointments with all,
>> I will not have a single person slighted or left away,
>> The keptwoman and sponger and thief are hereby invited . . .
> the heavy-lipped slave is invited. . . . the venerealee is invited,
>> There shall be no difference between them and the rest.

The Eucharist, therefore, is not simply a *symbolic* expansion of the moral circle. The Lord's Supper becomes a profoundly subversive political event in the lives of the participants. The sacrament brings real people—divided in the larger world—into a sweaty, intimate, flesh-and-blood embrace where "there shall be no difference between them and the rest."

4.

But as we observed with Peter, this embrace is difficult to maintain. If the Lord's Supper is pushing against innate and deeply entrenched psychological tendencies (tendencies producing otherness and exclusion) there is always the temptation that these tendencies will, either willfully or unconsciously, win out and reassert themselves, importing the sociomoral boundaries from the culture into the life of the church. It seems that something very much like this had occurred in the church of Corinth.

My analysis of the situation in Corinth will lean heavily on Ben Witherington's excellent and influential treatment *Conflict and Community in Corinth*. Following Witherington, it seems clear that one of the problems in Corinth was the rift between the rich and the poor within the church. In various ways the wealthy and privileged patrons of the church of Corinth were causing problems for both Paul and the poorer members of the church. This can be seen in a variety of places in 1 Corinthians. For example, some of the wealthier members had been offended that Paul, during his time in the city, had refused their patronage and instead supported himself by working with his hands. No doubt this was intentional on Paul's part, an attempt to identify with the poor in the city and the church. As Witherington writes:

> Well-to-do or aristocratic Romans, like Greeks, often had a low opinion of those who practiced a trade, and many of Paul's problems in Corinth seem to have been caused by the wealthy and the social climbers among Corinthian Christians who were upset at him for not meeting their expectations for a great orator and teacher . . . In a city where social climbing was a major preoccupation, Paul's deliberate stepping down in apparent status would have been seen by many as disturbing, disgusting, and even provocative.[6]

Socioeconomic tensions between the Corinthian members themselves were also causing problems. For example, Paul condemns the Corinthians for taking each other to public court to seek legal resolutions to their disputes. Generally, only the rich and privileged could expect justice from the Roman court system. Thus, we can assume that rich Christians were taking the poorer members of the church to court in the expectation of a favorable verdict.

6. Witherington, *Conflict and Community*, 20, 21.

Additional rich/poor fissures in the Corinthian church occurred over eating meat sacrificed to idols. Most poor Christians would not have had regular access to meat. The meat the lower classes did eat was often the meat made available to the public during the pagan religious festivals. Thus, for poor Christians meat was strongly associated with pagan religion, the life they renounced when they joined the Christian community. By contrast, the rich were able to eat meat more regularly, being able to buy and prepare meat in their own homes. Thus, for the rich the meat/temple association was weakened over time. This created the clash of "consciences" in the Corinthian church. As Witherington notes:

> Probably, as Theissen suggests, "the weak" in Corinth are poor Christians for whom *eidolothuta* [idol food] was especially likely to have religious associations, because they had eaten it before only at some public temple feast for a holiday in the temple. This would explain their strong scruples.[7]

But the rich/poor fissure that particularly interests us was the behavior of the Corinthian church during the Lord's Supper. Again, as a lived expression of Jesus' inclusive fellowship, the rich and the poor in Corinth were to welcome each other and step into the egalitarian embrace of the Lord's Table. But something, as we have seen, was amiss in Corinth. The wealthy members were, in various ways, expressing contempt for the poor in the church. Thus, it comes as no surprise that the experience of the Lord's Supper became exclusive rather than inclusive. Paul describes the situation in chapter 11:

> In the following directives I have no praise for you, for your meetings do more harm than good. In the first place, I hear that when you come together as a church, there are divisions among you, and to some extent I believe it. No doubt there have to be differences among you to show which of you have God's approval. When you come together, it is not the Lord's Supper you eat, for as you eat, each of you goes ahead without waiting for anybody else. One remains hungry, another gets drunk. Don't you have homes to eat and drink in? Or do you despise the church of God and humiliate those who have nothing? What shall I say to you? Shall I praise you for this?

7. Ibid., 190.

> Certainly not! . . . So then, my brothers, when you come to-
> gether to eat, wait for each other.

What, exactly, was going on in Corinth during the Lord's Supper? It seems clear that the rich/poor "divisions" were causing a failure to "wait for each other" during the Lord's Supper. This "failing to wait" was causing some Christians to become well fed and drunk while others were going hungry. These actions functioned in some way to "humiliate those who have nothing." People were being shamed and embarrassed by the contempt being shown them.

What was going on? The situation is clarified somewhat if we consider aspects of Roman dining practices. As Witherington discusses, it appears that the Corinthian church was treating its communal meal, eaten prior to the celebration of the Lord's Supper, as a private dinner party followed by a *convivium* (i.e., drinking party). It was normal practice in Roman dinner and drinking parties to rank guests according to social status. Generally, high status guests ate with the host in a separate room where they were served first and were given the best food and drink. Lower status guests were seated elsewhere in the house, were served last, and were served food of lesser quality.

It appears that the wealthy patrons of the Corinthian church had imported these social practices into the life of the church. During the communal meal the church was segregated, with the wealthy Christians gathered in a separate room with the host. There, food was served (along with after-dinner drinking) with little regard as to the situation elsewhere in the house where the poorer Christians were being served, if at all. Further, the order of service had the wealthier patrons of the church eating first and well into their drinking party before lower-status members of the church had been served in the far reaches of the house. Although the notion of "wait for" could apply to the order of food service, Witherington notes that the word *ekdechomai* often has the sense of "welcome" and "hospitality."[8] That is, what was bothering Paul was less the issue of who was served first but the separation, segregation, privileging, and hierarchical nature of the gathering. This is clear in Paul's concern over "differences." The word for "differences" is *haireseis*, from which we get our word *heresy*. The later technical definition of heresy was a difference of

8. Ibid., 248–49.

belief, but the original and more primitive notion of heresy was *socio-logical division and exclusion.* The Corinthian Christians were *heretical* in how they were erecting divisions between themselves.[9]

It also seems clear that the emotion of contempt was driving these divisions within the Corinthian church. We know this because Paul explicitly takes up the issues of honor and shame in chapter 12. In chapter 12 Paul offers up his famous "body metaphor" of the church, illustrating the relationship of the various "members" to the "one body." Importantly for our purposes, Paul's interest in using this metaphor is not simply to highlight the diversity of gifts in the church but also to clarify how we are to treat "body parts" (i.e., people, most likely the poor members of the church) that are considered to be more shameful, dishonorable, or unpresentable:

> The eye cannot say to the hand, "I don't need you!" And the head cannot say to the feet, "I don't need you!" On the contrary, those parts of the body that seem to be *weaker* are indispensable, and the parts that we think are *less honorable* we treat with special honor. And the parts that are *unpresentable* are treated with special modesty, while our *presentable* parts need no special treatment. But God has combined the members of the body and has *given greater honor to the parts that lacked it,* so that there should be *no division in the body,* but that its parts should have equal concern for each other.

It seems clear that, for Paul at least, the divisions in the church were being caused by contempt and disgust. Some members of the Corinthian church were not "honorable" or "presentable." Paul's reference to genitalia is striking. The genitalia are "not presentable" and are covered up in public out of modesty. On its face, this metaphor might seem to reinforce the instincts of the wealthy patrons at Corinth, that the poor members were shameful. These feelings could be taken as justification for having these poor people "hidden away" in the far reaches of the house during the Lord's Supper. And yet, Paul flips the meaning of this metaphor in a powerful way. If some members are "unpresentable" (akin to genitalia) they should not be treated with shame, disgust, or contempt. Rather, is not our covering up of our "private parts" a sign that these parts require special attention, care, and treatment? Paul is arguing that, rather than expelling,

9. Ibid., 248. Italics are mine

hiding, or marginalizing these "less presentable" members, *special at-tention* should be given to care for, honor, and include these members in the body. Only then will there be "no divisions in the body." As Witherington observes, the Lord's Supper in the church at Corinth was meant to function as a form of resistance to the contempt-based stratification inherent in Roman society:

> In many ways [a Roman] meal was an occasion for gaining or showing social status. And it might be in many regards a microcosm of the aspirations and aims of the culture as a whole. Paul's attempt to deconstruct the social stratification that was happening in the Lord's Supper goes directly against the tendency of such meals . . . the sacred tradition concerning the Lord's Supper is recited specifically to encourage social leveling, to overcome factionalism created by stratification and its expression at meals, and to create unity and harmony in the congregation.[10]

In short, the Lord's Supper was the realization of new social and political arrangements, the embodiment of the social leveling seen in Jesus' ministry, most profoundly in his acts of table fellowship. Importantly, as we have seen, these new social arrangements could only be achieved if the emotions of social stratification were confronted, eliminated, or reinterpreted. In his body metaphor, Paul dramatically reframes these *heretical emotions*, the emotions of contempt, disgust, honor, and social presentability. Rather than signaling exclusion and division—the natural expulsive impulse inherent in these emotions—Paul suggests that these emotions should signal just the opposite in the Kingdom of God: honor, care, and embrace.

10. Ibid., 244, 245.

8

Hospitality and Embrace

Practice hospitality.

—Romans 12.13b

In our extended examination of sociomoral disgust in Part 3, we have been exploring the psychological dynamics of social exclusion, rejection, and expulsion. A key observation has been the recognition that disgust and love are reciprocal processes. Disgust is the primary process erecting boundaries between the self and the world. Love is a secondary process that allows others access to the "territory of the self." This access is physical (allowing kinds of physical touch, intimacy, or proximity), social (creating intimate webs of friends and family), behavioral (allowing people inside one's moral circle and granting them special claims on our time, effort, and resources), and emotional (granting access to warmth and acceptance within our hearts and minds).

Opposed to the forces of exclusion are the impulses of inclusion, welcome, and embrace. Within the Christian tradition these are the practices of hospitality. Having considered the psychological dynamics that undermine the practices of welcome, I would like to end Part 3 by examining hospitality as a positive action and to address objections that might be leveled at the analyses offered across the last few chapters.

1.

It could be argued that hospitality—the welcoming of strangers—is the quintessential Christian practice. Welcoming sinners to table fellowship was a central, distinctive, and perhaps the most inflammatory aspect of Jesus' ministry and teaching. Further, the gospel writers often create an identity relationship between Jesus and strangers. This identification—God as the stranger—echoes the story told in Genesis 18 in which Abraham extends hospitality to three strangers collectively identified as "the Lord." This story shaped the imagination of the early Christians as seen in the admonition of Heb 13:2, a reference to Genesis 18, to "not forget to entertain strangers, for by so doing some people have entertained angels without knowing it."

In the gospels, for example Matt 25:34–40, Jesus explicitly identifies himself with the stranger and overtly links the ethic of the Kingdom with acts of hospitality:

> Then the King will say to those on his right, "Come, you who are blessed by my Father; take your inheritance, the kingdom prepared for you since the creation of the world. For I was hungry and you gave me something to eat, I was thirsty and you gave me something to drink, I was a stranger and you invited me in, I needed clothes and you clothed me, I was sick and you looked after me, I was in prison and you came to visit me."
>
> Then the righteous will answer him, "Lord, when did we see you hungry and feed you, or thirsty and give you something to drink? When did we see you a stranger and invite you in, or needing clothes and clothe you? When did we see you sick or in prison and go to visit you?"
>
> The King will reply, "I tell you the truth, whatever you did for one of the least of these brothers of mine, you did for me."

Elsewhere in the gospels welcoming children is considered to be an act of welcoming Jesus (cf. Matt 18:5). The Parable of the Good Samaritan, one of the clearest articulations of Jesus' ethic, is also a story about hospitality.

The resurrection narratives also explore the theme of Jesus as stranger. The Resurrected Lord consistently goes unrecognized in the resurrection narratives. The most striking example of this is found in the road to Emmaus narrative (Luke 24) where two followers of Jesus encounter the resurrected Christ but fail to recognize him.

Intriguingly, in Luke 24 Christ is revealed to these followers in the act of hospitality. The Resurrected Lord is *known* by extending hospitality to a stranger.

Given all this, and combined with the central place of table fellowship in Jesus' ministry, it is not surprising that hospitality was a defining feature and virtue of the early church (cf. Acts 2:42–47, 4:32–37; 1 Tim 3:2, 5:10; 1 Pet 4:9; Titus 1:8; Rom 12:13, 15:7). As Christine Pohl notes in her book *Making Room*, these practices continued to be a distinctive feature of Christian communities during the first centuries of the church:

> Hospitality to needy strangers distinguished the early church from its surrounding environment. Noted as exceptional by Christians and non-Christians alike, offering care to strangers became one of the distinguishing marks of the authenticity of the Christian gospel and of the church. Writing from the first five centuries demonstrate the importance of hospitality in defining the church as a universal community, in denying the significance of the status boundaries and distinctions of the larger society, in recognizing the value of every person, and in providing practical care for the poor, stranger, and sick.[1]

If hospitality is a defining, central, and quintessential facet of Christian mission, then we learn something about the shape and character of sin and brokenness in human affairs. Specifically, what is so special about extending welcome? What wound is being attended to in the act of hospitality? What sin is being challenged and redeemed?

Our analysis of sociomoral disgust suggests that sin is often characterized by the forces of dehumanization. These forces may be subtle or shockingly brutal. But they all share a common core: the stratification of humanity along a divinity dimension with superior groups (defined as "my tribe") elevated over other ("outside") groups. These forces of dehumanization affect how we treat others (e.g., the moral circle), how we select scapegoats, and how we choose who is worthy of love and affection.

Given the impact of sociomoral disgust upon human affairs, it is not surprising that the act of hospitality is fundamentally an act of human recognition and embrace. If exclusion is fundamentally

1. Pohl, *Making Room*, 33.

dehumanizing, hospitality acts to restore full human status to the marginalized and outcast. As Pohl writes:

> For much of church history, Christians addressed concerns about recognition and human dignity within their discussion and practices of hospitality. Especially in relation to strangers, hospitality was a basic category for dealing with the importance of transcending social differences and breaking social boundaries that excluded certain categories or kinds of persons . . . Hospitality resists boundaries that endanger persons by denying their humanness.[2]

As we have observed repeatedly here in Part 3, sociomoral disgust is a psychological force that denies the "humanness" of others. Sociomoral disgust creates the "social boundaries that exclude certain categories or kinds of persons." In this we see how sociomoral disgust and the practices of hospitality are opposing forces within the life of the church. Unfortunately, sociomoral disgust, as we observed in Part 2, is deeply implicated in how we experience purity and holiness. The quest for holiness pushes against hospitality, prompting withdrawal, expulsion, and quarantine. Once again we encounter the conflict between *mercy*—the practices of hospitality—and *sacrifice*, what Volf has called "the will to purity."

This understanding should make it clear that Christian hospitality is not the watered down notion we observe in the "hospitality industry." Hospitality isn't simply a warm greeting. As we observed in the church at Corinth, the Lord's Supper and the hospitality associated with it was a deeply countercultural act in the life of the early church. Sociomoral borders, often associated with socioeconomic disparities, were challenged and dismantled. Hospitality is politically subversive. This explains the inflammatory nature of Jesus' ministry of table fellowship. Eating with tax collectors and sinners was an attack upon the status quo. As Pohl observes, "hospitality is resistance":

> Because the practice of hospitality is so significant in establishing and reinforcing social relationships and moral bonds, we notice its more subversive character only when socially undervalued persons are welcomed. In contrast to a more tame hospitality that welcomes persons already well situated in a community, hospitality that welcomes "the least" and recognizes their equal

2. Ibid., 62, 64.

value can be an act of resistance and defiance, a challenge to
the values and expectations of the larger community.[3]

Beyond resistance, hospitality also has a remedial function.
Where people are abandoned, socially or economically, hospitality
seeks to provide human affection and material care. In extreme cases,
hospitality provides refuge for the victims of society. During WWII
German citizens and entire towns provided sanctuary and refuge for
their Jewish neighbors. In America the hosts of the Underground
Railroad provided haven and care for slaves seeking freedom.

In all of this we see how the practice of hospitality is the an-
tithesis of sociomoral disgust. Where the dynamics of disgust and
dehumanization foster exclusion and expulsion, the practice of hospitality welcomes the outcast and stranger as a full member of the
human community. Hospitality seeks to expand the moral circle, to
push back against the innate impulse that assumes "humanity ends
at the border of the tribe." A final word from Pohl:

> Strangers, in the strict sense, are those who are disconnected
> from basic relationships that give persons a secure place in the
> world. The most vulnerable strangers are detached from family,
> community, church, work, and polity. This condition is most
> clearly seen in the state of homeless people and refugees. Others
> experience detachment and exclusion to lesser degrees.
>
> When we offer hospitality to strangers, we welcome them
> into a place to which we are somehow connected—a space that
> has meaning and value to us. This is often our home, but it also
> includes church, community, nation, and various other institu-
> tions. In hospitality, the stranger is welcomed into a safe, per-
> sonal, and comfortable place, a place of respect and acceptance
> and friendship. Even if only briefly, the stranger is included in a
> life-giving and life-sustaining network of relations.[4]

2.

Given this call to hospitality, it is time, here at the end of Part 3, to
face objections to the argument being offered. Specifically, if love

3. Ibid., 62.
4. Ibid., 13.

involves the eradication of boundaries are we not left, psychologically and communally, in a very dangerous situation? Boundaries of selfhood and community are vital to maintaining psychological and communal integrity. At the end of the day, disgust is a protective mechanism. Thus, any assault on disgust and the practices of purity needs to face these dangers honestly and candidly. Broadly, there are two major objections to a call for radical embrace and hospitality. The first objection expresses psychotherapeutic concerns. The second objection is ecclesial in nature. But both share a common core concern: a worry about issues related to *integrity*, psychological and communal. I'll address the psychotherapeutic issues first and conclude Part 3 with a discussion of the ecclesial concerns.

3.

One of the key insights we have gained in our examination of disgust is how disgust is, inherently, a boundary psychology. In the social realm, disgust then functions as an emotion of otherness, exteriority, and alterity. The effects of disgust range from the subtle to the genocidal. And as the infrahumanization research revealed, disgust processes affect us all, regulating how we reason about and experience group membership in everyday interactions. We all have a moral hitch in our hearts, a slight hesitancy to grant out-group members full human status. Too often, humanity, even if only subtly, ends at the border of our tribe. For the most part, these tendencies can only be detected in reaction time tests, but their mere existence allows hate, discrimination, scapegoating, and paranoia to take hold in a population during times of communal stress.

Given this dynamic, we observed how love involves the dissipation of the emotions of otherness. This entails the dismantling of cognitive and emotional boundaries between the self and the other. We call this emotional identification "love" or "intimacy."

It is at this point that certain psychotherapeutic objections are raised. All this talk about dismantling or dissolving the boundaries between self and other tends to fly in the face of certain psychotherapeutic recommendations that suggest that proper "boundaries" between the self and others are vital for emotional and relational well-being. There may be fears that the analysis I'm offering, that love dismantles boundaries of selfhood, could create enmeshment and dependency. That is, it is often argued that psychological and relational health requires clear and appropriate boundaries between self and other. These boundaries create a space for self-care and emotional restoration: we disengage from others to care for the self. The worry is that if boundaries between the self and other don't exist then the self would be worn down, expended, or victimized by the relational demands of others. Clear "boundaries" prevent this from happening. So the objection is, given all this talk about dismantling psychological boundaries between self and other, am I not recommending a variety of unhealthy and pathological processes?

I'd like to respond to this criticism in a couple of different ways. To begin, I'd like to simply assert that my descriptions of love are demonstrably true, uncontroversial, and widely recognized. Recall, I've claimed that in love the self and the other become so identified, emotionally and symbolically, that the two form a union, an identification, a fusion. This might seem like the very definition of enmeshment but, upon consideration, this description of love describes how most of us do, in fact, experience love. Consider the love between a parent and a child. What parent, if faced with the choice, wouldn't sacrifice the use of his or her right arm to save their child? Or even give their very life? The point is that the safety and well-being of the child is more important than the parent's own physical body. This, after all, is what we mean by sacrificial love: the loss of the self (e.g., one's own life or situation in the world) for the sake of the other. And this loss of self doesn't have to be a dramatic life or death choice. Parents frequently forgo life opportunities and their own ambitions to make sure that their children have the chance for a better life. In all of this we see how our notions of selfhood become intertwined and fused with the other to the point where *the well-being of the other is how I define my selfhood!* Anyone who loves understands this. What is radical about the call of Jesus is that he extends this love not just to children and family but to the entire world, friends and enemies alike.

In short, I'd like to stand by the claim that love involves a cognitive and emotional identification, the dissipation of the psychological boundaries between self and other. So much so that, yes, the "self" might be sacrificed or "lost" in the act of love. But if this is the case, how are we to approach the psychotherapeutic concerns about unhealthy boundaries, enmeshment, victimhood, and dependency?

I think the first thing to say is that the psychotherapists are thinking about what we might call a morbid situation. That is, their concern over boundaries comes from a situation, the therapy room, where relationships are often found to be diseased, dysfunctional, or maladaptive. Very often these relational dysfunctions are produced by a morbid self-concept. Having low self-esteem, people seek affirmation from others. Or they may fail to object to (or even notice) abuse from others. Due to a morbid self-concept the individual allows the other to "use and abuse" them. To protect against this, the psychotherapeutic recommendation is to establish boundaries between self and other. The individual is encouraged to push back on the demands of the other to allow the morbid self-concept room for self-care and rehabilitation.

This account seems reasonable and, in fact, is widely accepted in our culture. However, I have a number of concerns with this account as it stands. First, it seems clear that the psychotherapeutic concern over healthy boundaries has little to do with love as I have described it. Rather, the establishment of boundaries here signals the failure of love. Specifically, "healthy boundaries" are encouraged when the mutuality of love has been lost. The other (e.g., an abusive spouse) is actively hurting the individual. And the morbid self-concept of the person in therapy is allowing this abuse (in its many manifestations) to continue. Consequently, the therapist is keen to encourage the individual to erect emotional and behavioral "boundaries." But these boundaries are erected between the self and the other as a form of *protection*. And this recommendation is wholly consistent with the analysis of love I've presented. Boundaries act as a form of *separation* between the self and the other, often signaling the failure of love.

And this observation brings me to my second and more important worry concerning the psychotherapeutic critique. Specifically, and this is somewhat understandable, the psychotherapeutic community has tended to fetishize the notion of boundaries. And in this fetishization of boundaries, the psychotherapeutic community has, perhaps unwittingly for Christian therapists, incorporated some of the most toxic aspects of modernity into their views of mental and spiritual health. Specifically, many of these modern notions of selfhood are difficult to reconcile with Trinitarian notions regarding Christian community, love, and salvation.

The modern view of the self, the view that dominates within the psychotherapeutic community, is characterized by what Charles Taylor has called the "buffered self." For a variety of reasons, which Taylor describes in his book *A Secular Age*, the modern notion of self-hood became introverted and individualistic, the self as isolated and distinct ("buffered") from the world. The notion of a self-determined, isolated, autonomous ego is a ubiquitous feature within modernity. The buffered self is a critical feature in how we moderns view our social contract, politically and economically. Further, the self-focus inherent in the notion of the buffered self has been a driving force behind many of the trends we see in the rise of psychotherapy. Extreme introversion is seen in the rise of Freudian psychoanalysis, a prime example of the modern commitment to the buffered self. Consider also the psychotherapeutic concerns with self-esteem, self-improvement, self-help, and self-actualization. All these manifestations of the introverted individualism of the buffered self are enshrined in the language of mental health and psychotherapy. Consequently, I think it important to note that the worry over "boundaries" is taking place within this context and, as a consequence, may be doubling down on modern values that Christian psychotherapists might want to revisit or, at the very least, sharply criticize.

In short, I am very comfortable with the account of selfhood and otherness described here in Part 3. As a recommendation for self-protection in abusive situations, the concern over boundaries makes sense. However, I would worry if the focus upon boundaries becomes fetishized to the point where a distorted view of selfhood—the buffered self—becomes enshrined within Christian psychotherapy as the ideal for human selfhood, relationship, and love. Because any Christian notion of selfhood and love will seek to be a participation in the triune love of God, the mutual self-giving agape between Father,

Son, and Holy Spirit. The three "persons" of the Trinity are *one*. The Godhead is *communal*. This recognition is vital to how the Christian understands the notion of agape. Christian love is inherently communal and self-giving. It is a participation in the triune life of God. The early church was the flesh and blood manifestation of this love, the mutual self-giving between Father, Son, and Holy Spirit:

> All the believers were one in heart and mind. No one claimed that any of his possessions was his own, but they shared everything they had. With great power the apostles continued to testify to the resurrection of the Lord Jesus, and much grace was upon them all. There were no needy persons among them. For from time to time those who owned lands or houses sold them, brought the money from the sales and put it at the apostles' feet, and it was distributed to anyone as he had need. (Acts 4:32–35)

What we see in Acts 4 is a communal notion of identity ("one in heart and mind") expressed in agape, hospitality, and Christian koinonia fellowship. Koinonia is also how Paul describes the Lord's Supper in 1 Corinthians. These are the social, psychological, economic, political, moral, and liturgical expressions of the love and life of the triune God.

It is no surprise, then, that modern persons, being driven by notions of the buffered self, have difficulty understanding the life and love of the early church. How does the psychotherapeutic concern over "healthy boundaries" fit into Acts 4? This is not to say that therapeutic concerns about self-care are illegitimate. It is simply the recognition that modernity cannot meaningfully speak about love. Modernity can talk about "healthy relationships" and make numerous recommendations about how we ought to manage life across the boundaries of selfhood, about whether we should accept or reject the claims upon the self from other buffered selves. Modernity will, thus, use economic metaphors to help us track the "inflow" versus "outflow" across the boundary of the self. Healthy love in modernity is making sure our "love bank" gets enough "deposits" to offset the relational "investments" we make in others. But it is very difficult to see how this modern version of "love"—exchange across the boundaries of autonomous egos—bears any resemblance to the triune love of God and Christian agape. And it is not hard to see why. The modern notion of the buffered self is simply a manifestation of what Martin Luther called *incurvatus in se*, the self "curved inward" upon itself. *Incurvatus in se* suggests that human sinfulness is rooted in self-focus, self-absorption, and self-worship. Love is impossible in this condition. And modernity and much within modern psychotherapy simply exacerbates this curvature inward upon the self.

So I believe the version of love presented in Part 3—dismantling the boundaries of otherness—sits very comfortably with notions of love and selfhood informed by Trinitarian theology. Although psychotherapeutic calls for "healthy boundaries" are necessary at times, I don't think a sustained critique from this angle has any real purchase. If anything, Christian psychotherapies should strive to eliminate modern notions of selfhood from their interventions and replace them with paradigms rooted in Christian agape and Trinitarian theology.

4.

Mary Douglas in her book *Purity and Danger* argues that notions of purity are intimately associated with the process of categorization. That is, human communities impose order and structure upon a chaotic and messy reality in order to coordinate and regulate their social life. As Douglas writes:

> Ideas about separating, purifying, demarcating, and punishing transgressions have as their main function to impose system on an inherently untidy experience.[5]

Communal integrity is maintained by monitoring and preserving these classifications, keeping aspects of life distinct and separate. Notions of purity aid the community in monitoring these systems of classification. As Douglas writes, "Where there is no differentiation there is no defilement."[6] The system of differentiation creates the attribution of *dirt*: "Where there is dirt there is a system."[7] Dirt is the attribution that life has become "messy" and disordered, where aspects of life—physical or, more often, moral—have come into illicit

5. Douglas, *Purity and Danger*, 5.

6. Ibid., 198.

7. Ibid., 44.

contact, been *blended* or dissolved into an undifferentiated *mixture*. More specifically, dirt is transgressive; it signals a normative failure. In this, by linking normative failures to dirt, pollution, and contagion, powerful psychological systems are mobilized to enforce the norms of the community upon the wayward individual. Transgression becomes a form of pollution.

To prevent the experience of dirt and pollution—transgressive contact or mixing—taboos are erected to keep communal life from disintegrating back into a disordered and chaotic state. If taboos begin to fail and normative boundaries are regularly violated, there is the sense that the moral fabric of the society is disintegrating and that the categories that ordered life can no longer be counted on. The norms that protected the moral integrity of the community have been lost and now everything seems "up for grabs." In Nietzschean terms, a transvaluation of values is occurring. Douglas might say that the definition of "dirt" is shifting. Regardless, if the community is going to maintain coherence and integrity, new classifications need to be adopted.

The issue that Douglas helps us see is that purity is intimately associated with communal integrity, particularly normative integrity. At some point, the community will have to make distinctions, to draw lines in the sand to define its normative existence. That is to say, all communities will establish notions of dirt and pollution. Dirt, in fact, defines (negatively so) the normative core of the community, the shared assumptions about what is licit and illicit, about what is proper versus transgressive.

With these insights in hand we can understand the reaction of the Pharisees in Matthew 9. Jesus' ministry of table fellowship, by blurring the purity boundaries, was introducing a normative dirt into the life of the community. Things (people in particular) were not in their proper places. Illicit and transgressive mixing was occurring.

This brings us back to the notion of the monstrous. As we noted in Chapter 6, monsters are often illicit hybrids, the transgressive mixture of the holy and the unclean. In this, monsters symbolize dirt, the disordering of the normative categories of a settled communal existence. Monsters, by blurring the distinctions between man and animal, and the holy and vile, threaten the moral integrity of the community. Monsters signal the onset of the unholy and normative chaos. Monsters, in short, are dangerous.

And this brings us to the second criticism about the practices of hospitality and embrace. Should we extend hospitality to monsters? And if we do, are we not courting the danger inherent in the monstrous, the blurring and failure of normative distinctions that define and protect the moral integrity of the group? Phrased differently, a community that embraces everything fails to be any community at all. As Douglas helps us see, dirt defines community.

Sociomoral disgust is an attempt to protect the group from toxic membership. As we have seen, all too often these attempts at protecting the group backfire. In extreme cases, these efforts at self-preservation lead to scapegoating violence. In milder forms it simply preserves the status quo of current social arrangements. Consequently, we observed the ambivalent note running through monster stories, the worry that the monster is human, that the scapegoat is innocent.

But there are real monsters out there, real dangers to the physical and normative integrity of the group. Should, for example, churches extend hospitality to pedophiles in light of their responsibilities to the children and parents of the faith community? Less dramatic but more important for our purposes are threats to the *moral* and *spiritual* integrity of the group. How radical should hospitality be in extending embrace to sinners?

I was recently confronted anew by this question while reading the provocative parables of Peter Rollins in his book *The Orthodox Heretic*. In the book, Rollins gives us a parable of hospitality entitled "Salvation for a Demon."[8] The parable dramatically confronts us with the question of extending hospitality to monsters. It begins with a "kindly old priest" famous for his hospitality: "The priest welcomed all who came to his door and gave completely without prejudice or restraint. Each stranger was, to the priest, a neighbor in need and thus an incoming of Christ." All well and good until a demon knocks on the church door in the middle of the night on a cold winter evening. The demon asks the priest "Will you welcome me in?" so that it can rest from its travels. "Without hesitation" the priest welcomes the demon inside the church. Once inside the demon destroys the

8. Rollins, *Orthodox Heretic*, 24–29.

holy artifacts and spits out curses and blasphemies. All the while the priest calmly continues his evening devotions until it is time for him to retire to his home. The demon follows the priest to his home and asks if the priest would welcome him inside to share a meal. Again, the priest extends hospitality, welcoming the demon into his home and sharing his evening dinner with the demon. Inside the house and during the meal, the demon continues to destroy the religious artifacts found in the house and to spew curses and blasphemies. The priest remains calm and peaceful. Finally, in the climax of the parable, the demon makes one final request, a final test of the priest's hospitality:

> "Old man, you welcomed me first into your church and then into your house. I have one more request for you: will you now welcome me into your heart?"
>
> "Why, of course," said the priest, "what I have is yours and what I am is yours."
>
> This heart felt response brought the demon to a standstill, for by giving everything the priest had retained the very thing the demon sought to take. For the demon was unable to rob him of his kindness and his hospitality, his love and his compassion. And so the great demon left in defeat, never to return.
>
> . . . And the priest? He simply ascended this stairs, got into bed and drifted off to sleep, all the time wondering what guise his Christ would take next.

In his commentary on the parable, Rollins calls this a story of "radical, impossible hospitality," the hallmark of which is the unconditional embrace of the priest. Further, Rollins links his parable to the motifs we have observed in the monster story, the notion that the monster might not really be a monster at all. As Rollins concludes his commentary:

> To welcome the demon, in whatever form the demon takes, is all but impossible. But through our trying to show hospitality to the demon at our door, the demon may well be transformed by the grace that is shown. Or, we may come to realize that it was not really a demon at all, but just a broken, damaged person like ourselves.[9]

9. Ibid., 29.

No doubt there is a breathtaking and inspiring quality in this vision of radical, unconditional, and impossible hospitality. And much of what I have described in Part 3 could be read as an endorsement of just this sort of radical embrace, the complete dissolution of the boundary between the self and the other: welcoming the "demon," as dramatically illustrated by Rollins, "into our hearts."

And yet, numerous objections can be raised at this point. As the work of Mary Douglas highlights, communities require distinctions to maintain their normative integrity. Radical hospitality may be inspiring, but it is difficult to see how the community can maintain its ethical and spiritual peculiarity if no distinctions are made between the "demons" and the church. True, it might be claimed, the church is distinctive and peculiar in the act of radical hospitality. Where the world erects boundaries of otherness, the church is noteworthy for dismantling those boundaries. No doubt this vision of radical agape exerts a normative pull upon the church. But there are numerous instances in Scripture where concerns are voiced about the people of God "losing their saltiness," becoming "lukewarm," or becoming "polluted by the world." Suddenly, we find in all this concerns over purity and holiness—moral and spiritual integrity—reasserting themselves. The tensions between mercy and sacrifice never really go away. In short, will not radical hospitality come into conflict with the call to holiness, the impulse to be a "peculiar people" set apart from the world?

Despite the vision of radical hospitality in Matthew 9, we must squarely confront the fact that expulsive elements continued to be a feature in the early church. And, not surprisingly, these expulsive dynamics were involved in protecting the spiritual and moral integrity of the faith community. As we are now well aware at this point in our meditations, holiness will always have an expulsive facet. And expulsion can have a protective function. That is, after all, why disgust exists in the first place: to prevent us from incorporating something that can harm our health and life. Perhaps the clearest example of this protective function also comes from 1 Corinthians.

In 1 Corinthians 5, Paul addresses a case of sexual immorality (along with other moral infractions) within the church. A male member of the church had "taken his father's wife." Despite this egregious moral failure, the Corinthians were continuing to associate with this man. More, the Corinthians seemed "proud" in this behavior, perhaps congratulating themselves on their inclusive and tolerant big-heartedness. Paul, deeply worried about preserving the moral integrity of the church, chastises the Corinthians and makes a variety of expulsive recommendations. The text is worth quoting in full for the contrast it provides with Rollins' parable of radical hospitality. I've highlighted the language of *sacrifice, expulsion,* and *quarantine*:

> It is actually reported that there is sexual immorality among you, and of a kind that does not occur even among pagans: A man has his father's wife. And you are proud! Shouldn't you rather have been filled with grief and have *put out of your fellowship* the man who did this? Even though I am not physically present, I am with you in spirit. And I have already passed judgment on the one who did this, just as if I were present. When you are assembled in the name of our Lord Jesus and I am with you in spirit, and the power of our Lord Jesus is present, hand this man over to Satan, so that the sinful nature may be destroyed and his spirit saved on the day of the Lord.
>
> Your boasting is not good. Don't you know that *a little yeast works through the whole batch of dough? Get rid of the old yeast* that you may be a new batch without yeast—as you really are. For Christ, our Passover lamb, has been *sacrificed.* Therefore let us keep the Festival, not with the old yeast, the yeast of malice and wickedness, but with bread without yeast, the bread of sincerity and truth.
>
> I have written you in my letter *not to associate with sexually immoral people*—not at all meaning the people of this world who are immoral, or the greedy and swindlers, or idolaters. In that case you would have to leave this world. But now I am writing you that *you must not associate with anyone* who calls himself a brother but is sexually immoral or greedy, an idolater or a slanderer, a drunkard or a swindler. With such a man *do not even eat.* (1 Cor 5:1–11)

This is an important passage to grapple with given how we have framed the events in Matthew 9 and have suggested that Jesus' ministry of table fellowship with "tax collectors and sinners" should be normative for the church. For here in Paul we encounter the exact opposite impulse: the movement *away* from table fellowship ("do not even eat with such a man") to preserve the *holiness* (spiritual integrity) of the church. How are we to reconcile Matthew 9 and I Corinthians 5?

I want to tread lightly here. Church traditions will vary widely in the practices they adopt to maintain spiritual and moral integrity. For example, in Chapter 7 my discussion of the Lord's Supper suggested that the Lord's Supper was to be the ritual reenactment of Jesus' ministry of table fellowship. However, pushing against this vision are those faith traditions who use the Lord's Supper as a regulatory mechanism. The practice of "closed" communion allows the faith community to regulate the spiritual and moral health of its members, granting access to the Lord's Table only after various hurdles (ritual and moral) have been cleared. These practices tend to be more informed by Paul's recommendations in 1 Corinthians 5 ("do not even eat with such a man") than Jesus' table fellowship with "tax collectors and sinners." And beyond the practices of the Lord's Supper, church traditions also vary widely in how they use other expulsive and regulatory practices (e.g., shunning, excommunication). Across all of these practices some critical questions are being asked: How do we engage in the practices of embrace and hospitality while maintaining our communal commitment to holiness? How do we balance mercy and sacrifice?

Although the conversations about expulsive or exclusive ecclesial practices can get sticky, I think we might benefit from having approached these issues through the literature of disgust. Specifically, as I've argued, a root tension between mercy and sacrifice is inherently *psychological* in nature. More specifically, we've discovered that the deep worry in expulsive practices concerns their dehumanizing potential, how sociomoral disgust corrupts the heart. That is, it seems clear that church communities must protect their spiritual and moral integrity. There will be boundaries. Or, as Mary Douglas suggests, there will be dirt, normative distinctions that can become blurred or transgressed. In light of this, the critical issue, given our analysis of disgust, becomes how those practices are affecting how we emotionally experience otherness. Specifically, have the practices of church discipline begun to affect, at the psychological level, the dynamics of love, mercy, and hospitality? As we now know, certain psychological features characterize love, the expression of a *deep* hospitality. The practices of embrace and hospitality are not simply physical rearrangements. There is a vast difference in receiving welcome, refuge, or table fellowship from chilly, hostile, and begrudging hosts versus the embrace of warm, affectionate, and big-hearted hosts. One can literally feel the difference. The call to hospitality is not simply a call to charity but is, rather, a call to remake the heart, my emotional stance toward otherness. And this has important implications for church discipline. Simply stated, 1 Corinthians 5 cannot be understood without understanding 1 Corinthians 13. Again, God desires mercy, not sacrifice.

The critical issue isn't, in the end, if the church should or should not protect its moral and spiritual "purity." The critical issue concerns the fundamental stance toward the other—the erring brother, the stranger on the doorstep, the "tax collectors and sinners." It seems clear that church discipline is needed to preserve the integrity of the community. But there is no way to faithfully implement Paul's directives until the matters of the heart are confronted. Acts of charity can be dehumanizing. Church discipline can be dehumanizing. Calls for holiness can be dehumanizing. The outcome of these actions pivot off the status of the heart.

So how should the heart of hospitality be characterized? What kind of heart can eliminate sociomoral fissures? What kind of heart allows us to preserve communal integrity without demonizing the other? What kind of heart allows us to strive for purity and holiness without descending into the practices of scapegoating? Toward an answer, I want to lean again on the treatment of Miroslav Volf in his book *Exclusion and Embrace*. Volf's work is congenial because his treatment prioritizes the psychological aspects of embrace as the way out of the mercy/sacrifice impasse. Volf explicitly contrasts the *nature of the human agent* (the psychological aspects of selfhood and otherness, our central concerns throughout Part 3) with mere *physical rearrangements* (e.g., the physical accommodations seen in hospitality and justice). Volf writes:

> I want to concentrate on social agents. Instead of reflecting on the kind of society we ought to create in order to accommodate individual or communal heterogeneity, I will explore *what kind of selves we need to be* in order to live in harmony with others.[10]

10. Volf, *Exclusion and Embrace*, 20–21. Italics in original.

This focus on selfhood dovetails nicely with our discussions of sociomoral disgust. Specifically, we've come to understand how sociomoral fissures, often driven by the psychology of disgust, are created within the heart. Consequently, if we are to create, following Volf, selves that can live in harmony with others, we need to address the psychological aspects of disgust and dehumanization. This will be a difficult task. Worryingly, as the research on infrahumanization revealed, many of these psychological dynamics are subtle and unconscious. And as noted in our discussion of monsters, our scapegoating practices are not often transparent. According to René Girard, the power of the gospels rests upon their exposure of the violent self-interest inherent in scapegoating. But this exposure, crystal clear to the reader of the gospel accounts, often eludes us in our daily lives. The call to hospitality will be superficial and fragile if it is not practiced by persons striving mightily to transform and reconfigure deeply entrenched psychological biases and impulses. More, these individuals will often be operating "in the dark," as it were. Sociomoral fissures are often unconscious and outside of awareness. True people of welcome will attempt to penetrate this darkness within themselves. But the self-deceit inherent in introspection means that much within our hearts will remain dark and impenetrable. This darkness will continue to unconsciously influence our emotions, judgments, and behavior. In short, the only way forward for people of hospitality will be the assumption that they are *psychologically compromised* in various ways *even when they don't feel compromised!* This skeptical stance toward the self may be the most important insight produced by our psychological approach.

Volf describes this vital characteristic less as a suspicion about the self than about our relation to the other, what Volf calls the "will to embrace." But the analyses are complementary. Volf describes the will to embrace as a stance prior to any judgment of the other. The will to embrace is the default stance, the foundational position of the Christian person. All judgments and actions flow from this will to embrace. It is both prior to and persisting alongside any actions done for the sake of the Kingdom, be these acts of hospitality, worship, mission, or church discipline. Volf describes the critical feature of the will to embrace:

> . . . the will to give ourselves to others and "welcome" them, to
> readjust our identities to make space for them, is prior to any
> judgment about others, except that of identifying them in their
> humanity. The will to embrace precedes any "truth" about oth-
> ers and any construction of their "justice." This will is abso-
> lutely indiscriminate and strictly immutable; it transcends the
> moral mapping of the social world into "good" and "evil."[11]

Again, it seems clear that Volf's will to embrace is addressing the
psychological issues we have been discussing. Embrace must be *deep*.
Further, it must be *prior to any judgments, moral or otherwise, we make
of persons*. Only then will the fundamental humanity of the person be
protected from the psychology of disgust and dehumanization. It is
true that questions of welcome and inclusion pose difficult issues of
discernment for the faith community. But before those arrangements
and accommodations are contemplated, the will to embrace must be
the communal starting point. No discussion of hospitality or church
discipline can commence until the will to embrace the dignity of others is firmly in place. That is the root lesson of Matthew 9: *No conversation about sin, purity, or holiness can begin until human dignity has
been secured beyond all question or doubt*. Discussions of purity and sin
cannot be *primary* discussions. For when the "will to purity" trumps
the "will to embrace" (when sacrifice precedes mercy), the gears of
sociomoral disgust begin to turn, poisoning the well of hospitality by
activating the emotions of otherness. In the desire to secure purity the
faith community will begin to turn *inward*. The moral circle *shrinks*.
The church begins to define its spiritual mission as the regulation
of purity boundaries within the membership and between outsiders.
Walls—ritual, physical, and psychological—are erected to protect and
quarantine the faith community. It is the communal manifestation of
incurvatus in se. The community has become curved in on itself.

5.

The call to hospitality is no easy practice. I have no simple recommendations that reconcile the practices of hospitality with the need
for communal integrity and holiness. But hospitality is not a bland

11. Ibid., 29.

sort of moral tolerance, a limp liberalism. Hospitality is, as Christine Pohl writes, fundamentally about *making room*. But this room, following Volf, is a space opened within the self. Hospitality is, at root, an emotional and psychological activity. It is a *will* to embrace. A will that actively seeks to overcome the emotions of otherness. Everything about human social and moral psychology narrows our moral circle. Our natural instincts assure us that humanity ends at the border of our tribe. Our affections follow our ontology. Kindness flows toward my kin, my kind. Beyond those borders are strangers and monsters. And our feelings toward these "outsiders" range from blank indifference, to disgust, to contempt, to hatred. Hospitality is the fight against these impulses. It is a deep psychological struggle, fought tooth and nail every second of the day, to make room for others within the borders of my selfhood. To create in my own heart and mind, as Volf describes, a *catholic* self. Rejecting the buffered self of boundaries, I become "curved outward" in a catholic, universal embrace of the other. These are the selves we seek to create was we gather around the Lord's Table. Where the church, in the words of Whitman, meets around a "meal pleasantly set" where "there shall be no difference between them and the rest." Hospitality is about selfhood. It is that space where the dignity of every human person is vouchsafed, embraced, and protected deep within the heart of the church.

PART 4

Mortality

. . . Love has pitched his mansion in
The place of excrement;
For nothing can be sole or whole
That has not been rent.

—W. B. Yeats

9

Body and Death

In the last analysis Christian theology must either
accept death as a part of life or abandon the body.

—**Norman O. Brown**

1.

We now enter Part 4—*Mortality*—where we begin to consider the
existential facets of disgust. Recall that disgust is a promiscuous emotion. Beyond revulsion toward foodstuffs, a wide range of stimuli can
elicit disgust. As described in Chapter 1, the following stimuli tend to
be reliable disgust stimuli for North Americans:

1. Food
2. Body products (e.g., feces, vomit)
3. Animals (e.g., insects, rats)
4. Sexual behaviors (e.g., incest, homosexuality)
5. Contact with the dead or corpses
6. Violations of the exterior envelope of the body (e.g., gore,
   deformity)
7. Poor hygiene
8. Interpersonal contamination (e.g., contact with unsavory
   persons)
9. Moral offenses[1]

1. Haidt et al., "Individual Differences," 701–13.

As we have noted, the psychologist Paul Rozin has grouped these stimuli into three broad disgust domains[2]:

1. *Core Disgust: Food*: Revulsion centered on eating and oral incorporation. The adaptive core of disgust.
2. *Sociomoral Disgust: Moral offenses, people*: Revulsion centered on moral failures and social groups. The facets of disgust discussed in Parts 2 and 3.
3. *Animal-Reminder Disgust: Gore, deformity, animals, hygiene, death*: Revulsion centered on stimuli that function as death/mortality reminders. The existential aspect of disgust. This will be our focus here in Part 4.

We began this book with an examination of the domain of core disgust. Specifically, we described the unique psychology associated with disgust with a particular focus on the contamination "logic" associated with the disgust response. This analysis was important because it illuminates, given the associations between disgust and purity, how many of us tend to reason about moral and social issues. Consequently, Parts 2 and 3 examined how disgust psychology is implicated in moral judgments and social exclusion. Reviewing Part 2, we discussed a variety of consequences that occur when disgust psychology regulates our moral experience. A quick survey of those consequences:

1. Disgust is an expulsive emotion. Thus, "moral purity" is attained (or maintained) by acts of separation, cleansing, and quarantine.
2. Purity metaphors activate the "magical thinking" of contamination logic. Thus, moral reasoning about "purity violations" is often irrational. For example, *contact* and *proximity* become important considerations. *Dose insensitivity* frames the violation in catastrophic terms. And purity violations are felt to be *permanent* and beyond rehabilitation.
3. The Macbeth Effect. Given the strong psychological association between physical cleansing and spiritual purity, laboratory studies have shown how acts of physical cleansing—ritual or real—can *replace* and *substitute* moral effort and repentance.

2. Rozin et al., "Disgust," 637–53.

Hand washing literally substitutes for acts of compassion and justice.

4. Although all sins are generally considered to be purity violations (given understandings of God's holiness in both the Old and New Testaments) some sin categories are uniquely structured by purity metaphors. Specifically, sexual sins are often regulated by the metaphor of "sexual purity." This uneven use of purity metaphors across the domain of sin behaviors may be one explanation for why certain sin categories are felt to be more toxic and severe within some faith communities. Purity sins tend to be unfairly and unreasonably stigmatized in these groups. This creates greater shame and self-loathing for certain classes of sin.

5. Finally, the disgust reaction in the face of purity violations leaves us communally dumbfounded. Debates about purity violations are often immune to rational conversation or discussion. This is due to the fact that people sit with different felt experiences regarding what is or is not improper, degrading, or illicit. A "feeling of wrongness" is the only warrant deployed and we are stuck if people don't share those feelings. This dumbfounding often occurs when conservatives and liberals discuss moral issues.

The list above reviews some of the important consequences noted in Part 2 regarding the influence of disgust upon moral reasoning and the experience of sin within the life of the church. In Part 3 we turned to the social side of sociomoral disgust in which disgust properties are applied to individuals and populations. In Part 3 we made the following observations about sociomoral disgust:

1. Although we all recognize extreme cases of sociomoral disgust in incidents of genocide and hate, we often fail to recognize that sociomoral disgust is affecting all of us and is an everyday affair. Examples of how social disgust affects daily social interactions: finding people "creepy" or "nauseating"; the experience of the moral circle (the flow of kindness); the psychology of infrahumanization ("humanity ends at the border of the tribe"); and the emotion contempt (often seen in social hierarchies).

2. Critically, it was observed that disgust and love are reciprocal processes. Disgust erects and monitors boundaries of the self, and love, as a secondary process, allows those boundaries to be dismantled or blurred. This is most clearly seen in physical intimacy, where access to the body is granted. But we also observe this boundary transgression when we allow people access to the sacred spaces of life: home, church, nation. It was also observed that the reciprocal nature of disgust and love greatly complicates simplistic formulae such as "love the sinner but hate the sin." That is, if the emotions of otherness (e.g., disgust, contempt) are in play, love is psychologically compromised. This was clearly observed in Gottman's research on marital distress. Love and revulsion work against each other.

3. Unless sociomoral disgust is addressed in the heart, efforts toward justice, hospitality, or charity will be, in the end, ineffective and distancing. The "will to embrace" must precede any judgments of the other. Embrace must be *deep* and should not be reduced to social or political rearrangements and accommodations.

2.

Having investigated the domains of core and sociomoral disgust, we now turn to the third and final disgust domain—animal-reminder disgust.

Beyond disgust centered on food, morality, or people, disgust is often elicited by stimuli that seem to function as death/mortality reminders. Events or stimuli that highlight the weakness, decay, or vulnerability of the body often activate disgust responses. For example, people often feel disgusted when they encounter the handicapped, the elderly, poor hygiene, body fluids, deformity, corpses, gore (blood or viscera), or animals. Although many of these stimuli are implicated as legitimate disease vectors, there seems to be more going on than a simple adaptive impulse to avoid eating something harmful.

In short, disgust appears to have an existential component. Our body-related disgust is not simply about cleanliness. Rather, disgust seems to be fending off some deeper anxieties and ambivalences, many of which cluster about the body and bodily functions. Something about the body seems improper, illicit, pornographic, degrading, and disgusting.

The existential psychologists have suggested that the body is disgusting because we experience it as an *existential predicament*. Although we relish in the body, we know that it will, one day, fail us. Thus, animal-reminder stimuli are pushed away as revolting and inappropriate for contemplation.[3]

The term "animal-reminder" is used to highlight the fact that humans feel that they are *dual* creatures, both animal *and* spiritual. Body *and* soul. To be clear, this isn't a philosophical conclusion, an embrace of Cartesian dualism (although it could be that). Rather, this feeling of body/spirit duality appears to be a universal human experience, most likely the product of how we reason about minds and objects (see Paul Bloom's book *Descartes' Baby* for a review of the relevant cognitive science). Regardless, in the face of this bifurcated experience fears cluster around the animal/physical aspects of the body as the body is subject to the forces of entropy, death, and decay. And when we highlight our commonality with animals often a feeling of disgust and degradation can sweep over us. Consider how many Christians react to the implications of Darwinian evolution. Evolution, by highlighting our connection with animals, is felt to be humiliating and degrading, an attack on human dignity.

Among the existential psychologists, no one has done a better job than Ernest Becker in describing the animal/spiritual paradox of human existence. From his magisterial book *The Denial of Death*:

> . . . the essence of man is really its *paradoxical* nature, the fact that he is half animal and half symbolic . . . This is the paradox: he is out of nature and hopelessly in it; he is dual, up in the stars and yet housed in a heart-pumping, breath-gasping body . . . His body is a material and fleshy casing that is alien to him in many ways—the strangest and most repugnant way being that it aches and bleeds and will decay and die. Man is literally split in two: he has an awareness of his own splendid uniqueness in that he sticks out of nature with a towering majesty, and yet he goes back into the ground a few feet in order blindly and dumbly to rot and disappear forever. It is a terrifying dilemma to be in and have to live with . . . The knowledge

3. Goldenberg et al., "Fleeing the Body," 200–218.

of death is reflective and conceptual, and animals are spared it.
They live and they disappear with the same thoughtlessness:
a few minutes of fear, a few seconds of anguish, and it is over.
But to live a whole lifetime with the fate of death haunting
one's dreams and even the most sun-filled days—that's something else.[4]

This offensive union—the attachment of our symbolic/spiritual
selves with a body—is also implicated in what we might call, following the psychodynamic psychologists, the "scandal of anality."[5]
That is, if humans feel like (or at least desire to be) spiritual, angelic,
god-like, and immortal beings then participation in basic metabolic
functions—eating and excreting—is experienced as offensive and illicit. Becker elaborates:

> Excreting is the curse that threatens madness because it shows
> man in his abject finitude, his physicalness, the likely unreal-
> ity of his hopes and dreams. But even more immediately, it
> represents man's utter bafflement at the sheer *non-sense* of cre-
> ation: to fashion the sublime miracle of the human face, the
> *mysterium tremendum* of radiant feminine beauty, the veritable
> goddess that beautiful women are; to bring this out of noth-
> ing, out of the void, and make it shine in noonday; to take
> such a miracle and put miracles again within it, deep in the
> mystery of eyes that peer out—the eye that gave even the dry
> Darwin a chill: to do all this, and to combine it with an anus
> that shits! It is too much. Nature mocks us . . .[6]

A wonderful example of the animal-reminder facet of disgust
and how it relates to human degradation and mortality is found in
an account from the Puritan leader Cotton Mather. Mather was urinating outside when a dog came up beside him and lifted his leg to
urinate. These were Mather's reflections while he and the dog stood
side by side, both urinating on the wall:

> I was once emptying the Cistern of Nature, and making Water
> at the Wall. At the same Time, there came a Dog, who did so
> too, before me. Thought I; "What mean and vile Things are
> the Children of Men, in this mortal State! How much do our
> natural Necessities abase us and place us in some regard, on the

4. Becker, *Denial of Death*, 26–27.

5. See ibid., 30–34 and Brown, *Life Against Death*, 179–304.

6. Becker, *Denial of Death*, 33–34.

Level with the very Dogs!" . . . Accordingly, I resolved, that it should be my ordinary Practice, whenever I step to answer the one or other Necessity of Nature, to make it an Opportunity of shaping in my Mind some noble, divine Thought.[7]

Note the conflation in Mather of mortality, disgust, metabolism, and animals. Mather finds the metabolic function of urinating disgusting and degrading. Why? Because it is a physical necessity of our "mortal state" that places us "on the Level with" animals. Disgust seems to be protecting Mather from an existential confrontation. We resist reminders that we are, indeed, *animals* with vulnerable bodies prone to illness, injury, age, and, eventually, death. As Martha Nussbaum observes:

Disgust pertains to our problematic relationship with our own animality. Its core idea is the belief that if we take in the animalness of animal secretions we will ourselves be reduced to the status of animals. Similarly, if we absorb or are mingled with the decaying, we will ourselves be mortal and decaying. Disgust thus wards off both animality in general and the mortality that is so prominent in our loathing of our animality.[8]

Given that "human disgust reactions are typically mediated very powerfully by the awareness of death and decay,"[9] Nussbaum echoes Becker's analysis that "human beings cannot bear to live with the constant awareness of mortality and of their frail animal bodies."[10] Thus, "self-deception may be essential in getting us through a life which is soon bound for death."[11] Disgust aids in the self-deception by prompting us to push the animal-reminder stimuli away, allowing for a quick restoration of our existential equanimity.

3.

It might be surprising to discover that disgust is an existential emotion. We tend to think that a confrontation with death would lead to

7. Lee, *Against the Protestant Gnostics*, 131.

8. Nussbaum, *Hiding*, 91.

9. Ibid., 91.

10. Ibid., 17.

11. Ibid., 17.

either anxiety (for obvious reasons) or anger ("Rage, rage against the dying of the light!"). So why would *disgust* be implicated in the confrontation with *death*? First, as seen above, many of the reminders of our mortal, animal natures (e.g., feces, corpses) are, in themselves, stimuli for core disgust. As vectors of disease these stimuli are already disgust triggers. Due to this preexisting association, existential concerns related to these same stimuli are easily folded into the emotion of disgust.

But the connection between disgust and death goes deeper. Recall that disgust regulates the divinity dimension in human experience. Feelings of disgust are triggered when something "high" or "holy" is degraded or profaned. Generally speaking, we tend to place the spiritual aspects of existence "high" on the divinity dimension. Conversely, things that are physical and animal are seen as "low" on the divinity dimension. Man is "over" the animals. We don't want people to "descend to the level of animals." This is the dynamic at the root of Becker's claim that humans are paradoxical. The spiritual, elevated, and "higher" aspects of experience are intertwined with our "lower" animal nature. Given that disgust regulates and monitors the movements of elevation and degradation on the divinity dimension, it is not surprising that reminders of our animal nature are often seen as vulgar, inappropriate, illicit, and revolting.

Evidence in support of this notion is observed in an interesting exception to disgust responses regarding bodily fluids. Specifically, all bodily fluids, except one, are reliable disgust stimuli. Blood, vomit, urine, semen, sweat, and puss, all are found, generally speaking, to be disgusting. The one exception is the bodily fluid that seems quintessentially human and spiritual: tears.[12] Given that tears are associated with the deepest and most profound human experiences, tears are considered to be a kind of *spiritual fluid*, a fluid that *separates* us from the animals rather than identifies us with them. Consequently, tears do not produce disgust. As a *spiritual* fluid unique to humans, tears are "high" on the divinity dimension. Urine, by contrast, is "low" on the divinity dimension as it is a fluid shared with all animals (cf. Cotton Mather making Water at the Wall).

12. Goldenberg et al., "I Am Not an Animal," 427–35.

4.

Before going on, I'd like to note that the disgust/death/body associations we are discussing are not hypothetical. Over the last ten years an impressive body of empirical work has established these associations across a variety of laboratory tests. For example, empirical work has strongly linked body ambivalence to death concerns. Further, sensitivity to animal-reminder disgust has also been associated with mortality concerns.

In sum, as surprising as this might be, disgust appears to be an *existential emotion*. This seems to be due to the fact that body-related stimuli appear to function as mortality reminders. Wanting to protect ourselves from these reminders, we experience disgust and revulsion and seek to push these stimuli away as inappropriate, indecent, illicit, or nauseating.

(I would like to pause here to clarify that disgust cannot be reduced to existential worries. People find stimuli disgusting for a wide variety of reasons. The claim here is simply that existential anxiety concerning the vulnerabilities of our bodies can, often surprisingly, be implicated in disgust responses, that disgust can act as an existential buffer. But it is important to stress that body-related anxiety and ambivalence are not reducible to mortality concerns. Nor is death anxiety the strongest factor in body ambivalence. Culture is by far the more important influence regarding how we feel about our bodies. And the body is not universally experienced as an existential predicament or conundrum. Many persons, cultures, and religious groups have very positive views of the body. In short, while many religious groups consider the body to be a location of temptation, depravity, and bestial impulses, many faith communities consider the body to be holy, good, and a location for spiritual exultation.)

5.

Those clarifications made, it does seem clear that the body is a regular locus of spiritual and existential befuddlement. And this existential analysis offers one explanation for why body ambivalence is so pervasive in many (if not all) religious traditions. If the body functions as an animal-reminder, a spiritually minded people could easily fall into the dualistic temptation of seeing routine metabolic activities (defecating, farting, burping) as degrading and vulgar. These activities act as an affront to our aspiration to climb spiritually "upward." The body is holding us back, spiritually speaking. It seems pornographic to drag our feces, sweat, and urine into the Holy of Holies. Should we not, then, try to leave these things behind? And if we can't, should we not create a quarantine around our animal-nature, refusing it access to holy and sacred spaces? For example, issues of propriety, hygiene, and dress are important affairs in many churches. Generally, the rationale offered for this fussiness and fastidiousness is that we are to offer God our "best," in dress, hygiene, and decorum. But our existential analysis suggests that something more might be rumbling beneath the surface. Behind the impulse to "clean up" there may be an attempt to refuse our animal nature access to the sacred space. Following Freud, we might call this fussy fastidiousness anal-*retentive*, a symptom of the scandal of anality. A collective pretending that the people sitting in the sanctuary are not metabolic animals.

6.

Having introduced the psychology of animal-reminder disgust, we can now ask, why is any of this of concern for the church?

In the remaining chapters of Part 4 I want to build up to an answer to that question. But it might be helpful to anticipate the shape of that answer here at the start. Specifically, if disgust is activated in the face of the sweat, grime, and blood of human existence, then our tendency will be to *pull back* from those aspects of life. More, this pulling back from the gritty physicality of life is experienced as a *divine* movement, the directive of God. Recall, pulling away from our animal dependencies is often experienced as a movement *upward* on the divinity dimension: away from the animal and toward the divine. Psychologically, we feel that purity and holiness is achieved by *removing ourselves from the gutter and waste*. This impulse also makes us want to *protect* God from the disgusting aspects of our bodies and existence. God needs to be *quarantined*.

But this movement is worrisome. In the impulse *to become holy* we move *away* from the more dirty aspects of the human predicament. In light of the Incarnation, the divine moving into the grit of life, this holiness via a flight from the body seems to be pulling us in the wrong direction. The church is *pulled away from life rather than toward a deeper participation.* Shockingly, and contrary to human expectation, God was born as a human being, covered in sweat, blood, and amniotic fluid. Everything about this scene is a disgust trigger. God is squeezed out into the world through a woman's birth canal, attached to her by an umbilical cord. In the Incarnation God crashes through the quarantine of holiness and purity erected around Him. Often, the church is found running the other way.

To follow God into the scandal of the Incarnation, the church will have to squarely confront its experience of disgust. And as we have observed, this movement will kick up issues related to degradation, propriety, dignity, and decorum. But, as we'll see, these concerns are often symptomatic of a deeper existential worry rumbling beneath the surface. That is, debates about propriety or dignity are often expressions of an unconscious refusal to admit or engage with the gritty physicality of the human predicament. As T. S. Eliot observed in *Sweeney Agonistes*:

> Birth, and copulation, and death.
> That's all the facts when you come to brass tacks;
> Birth, and copulation, and death.

Birth, sex, and death. Each graphically displays our animal nature and physical dependencies. And each is associated with disgust psychology, a psychology activated to protect us from the illicit and pornographic nature of the human predicament. And yet, human life revolves around these experiences. Birth, sex, and death—these are the "brass tacks" of human existence. The scandal of the Incarnation is the movement *down* into "birth, and copulation, and death." If so, can the church squarely face its existential squeamishness and follow God into these realities?

10

Sex and Privy

The whole problem with this idea of obscenity and indecency,
and all of these things—bad language and whatever—it's all caused
by one basic thing, and that is: religious superstition . . . that the
human body is somehow evil and bad and there are parts of it that
are especially evil and bad, and we should be ashamed. Fear, guilt,
and shame are built into the attitude toward sex and the body.

—George Carlin

1.

Over the last few chapters I've repeatedly pointed out how disgust
protects the sacred and the holy from descending into the vulgar
and profane. A peculiar aspect of this phenomenon, one we have
hinted at but not yet fully analyzed, is how the body becomes identified as unclean and illicit. But why should the body be experienced
as degrading? We all have bodies, so the experiences of sex, urina-
tion, and defecation are universal and shared experiences. So why
pretend, particularly in public and sacred spaces, that such experiences do not exist?

Consider the case of Martin Luther. One of the joys of reading Luther is his refreshing honesty about the life of the body.
Consequently, it comes as no surprise that when Luther described the
moment when he first grasped the doctrine of "justification by faith"

he adds some candid details about the location of this revelation. In Luther's own words:

> These words "just" and "justice of God" were a thunderbolt to my conscience. They soon struck terror in me who heard them. He is just, therefore, He punishes. But once when in this tower I was meditating on these words, "the just lives by faith," "justice of God," I soon had the thought whether we ought to live justified by faith, and God's justice ought to be the salvation of every believer, and soon my soul was revived. Therefore it is God's justice which justifies us and saves us. And these words became a sweeter message for me. This knowledge the Holy Spirit gave me on the privy in the tower.[1]

Luther had his great insight, this theological thunderbolt, while defecating in the tower privy. In the years to follow, many Lutheran historians worked to "clean up" this image. It seemed scandalous that the great insight of the Protestant faith had occurred during a bowel movement. Should not this insight have occurred while Luther sat in his study hunched over the epistle to the Romans? Wouldn't this have been a more *appropriate* location and posture for such a wondrous spiritual revelation?

This impulse to sanitize Luther is the scandal of anality. Something high, spiritual, and holy is scandalously connected with a body that shits. Thus efforts are taken, as seen in early biographies of Luther, to separate and quarantine the spiritual from the physical. The connection between the *privy* and *spirituality* disgusts us. And motivated by that disgust we move away from the world hoping to become "clean" and more "spiritual." To be "holy" is to deny the privy.

But as Freud noted, we are "born between urine and feces." These are the "brass tacks" of human existence. Yet humans, aspiring to be like the angels, find this situation uncomfortable, inappropriate, and scandalous. At root, the scandal has to do with the existential predicament presented to us by the human body. We are troubled by aspects of the body that link us to our animal nature, the aspects of our bodily existence that remind us of our need, dependency, vulnerability, and mortality. As the psychological research revealed in the last chapter, death is often the worm at the core of body ambivalence.

1. Brown, *Life Against Death*, 202.

This dynamic creates problems for the church and her mission in the world. The church, propelled by disgust, flees and abandons the world. Or, if the church remains in the world, it erects purity quarantines around its life and consciousness. Stanley Hauerwas has remarked that the spiritual life of Christianity is very often "too spiritual." In the rush toward spirituality the body and the physical world is left behind. Much of this flight from the gritty physicality of life is motivated by existential fears.

2.

Still, some might resist the contention that the body is experienced as an existential predicament. Might a person simply assert that they find references to feces, sex, and urine to be *intrinsically* disgusting and vulgar, particularly in sacred contexts? Death, it might be claimed, has nothing to do with it. Recall in Chapter 4 when I discussed the outrage in my church when I used the word "crap" during a worship service. This was, in a mild way, another example of the sandal of anality. The purity quarantine of the sanctuary had been violated. The anger at my word choice was overtly centered on issues of decorum and propriety. Death anxiety, it would seem, had nothing to do with the response of the church. But if the existential psychologists are to be believed, death anxiety is often implicated in these responses, the anxious effort to keep the privy and the sacred separate. No doubt I would have been hard-pressed to convince an angry parishioner that death anxiety was implicated in his offense at the word "crap." But the link exists, as I'll try to show in this chapter, even if it goes unrecognized. The importance of this analysis is that it can help us come to grips with our feelings surrounding indecency and vulgarity. Those feelings are not always what we take them to be. As a result, until we fully come to grips with our feelings surrounding the illicit and taboo, we may, in our effort to sanitize our spiritual lives, refuse God full access to the world. We become "too spiritual" and deny the truth of the Incarnation. For if God cannot be at work in the privy, then where else has God been banished? What other dirty, disgusting places are quarantined off from the divine?

Note that this is not a call to throw open the doors of the church to every worldly, degrading influence. Again, disgust is a protective emotion, alerting us to potential danger. We discussed these dangers at the end of Part 3. But we should not follow disgust blindly. Our emotional reactions concerning degradation are complicated and require careful discernment. Many of our reactions regarding the profane and the vulgar are forms of denial, fear, and delusion, an effort to pretend that we are angels—to deny that bodies and privies exist.

3.

The great American philosopher regarding obscenity and vulgarity was the late comedian George Carlin. As seen in the quote at the start of this chapter, Carlin links notions of indecency to religious views of the body, "that the human body is somehow evil and bad and there are parts of it that are especially evil and bad, and we should be ashamed." More, "fear, guilt, and shame are built into the attitude toward sex and the body."[2]

But Carlin's analysis is incomplete. If certain body parts are "especially evil," no account is given as to why this should be the case. Sex and other bodily functions are natural and universal. Why set these functions and body parts apart? If the existential psychologists are to be believed, these are the body parts that function as animal and mortality reminders. But is this true? Do sex and defecation remind us of our mortality? The answer, surprisingly, is yes.

To illustrate the links between the body and death I'd like to discuss two pieces of research involving attitudes about sex and taboo language. The two cases are related. For example, the strongest expletive in American English—the f-word—is a reference to sex. And sex is often considered to be "dirty" and "vulgar."

So let's begin with sex. Is mortality awareness associated with sex? The Freudian psychodynamic tradition certainly felt there was an association between sex and death, with Freud famously positing sex and death as prime movers within the human psyche. And a historical survey of death attitudes and imagery in Western cultures

2. Breznican, "George Carlin Responds," (2004, March 13).

supports the naturalness of the death/sex association. For example, Philippe Ariès in his influential treatment *Western Attitudes Toward Death* describes many of the historical associations between sex and death in Western culture. Here is Ariès on death imagery in the sixteenth through eighteenth centuries:

> At the end of the fifteenth century, we see the themes concerning death begin to take on an erotic meaning. In the oldest dances of death, Death scarcely touched the living to warn him and designate him. In the new iconography of the sixteenth century, Death raped the living. From the sixteenth to the eighteenth centuries, countless scenes or motifs in art and literature associate death with love, Thanatos with Eros. These are eroticomacabre themes . . .[3]

These associations have carried into the modern period. For example, the death/sex association is graphically on display in modern film, fiction, music, television, video games, and graphic novels. With the rise of extremely violent films we now recognize the genre of "torture porn," in which we watch implacable killers, the personification of Death, chase screaming, scantily clad girls. In his famous essay *The Pornography of Death*, Geoffrey Gorer compares sexual pornography with the modern horror genre (film, graphic novels, and books):

> Neither type of fantasy [horror or pornography] can have any real development, for once the protagonist has done something, he or she must proceed to do something else, with or to someone else, more refined, more complicated, or more sensational than what occurs before. This somebody else is not a person; it is either a set of genitals, with or without secondary sexual characteristics, or a body, perhaps capable of suffering pain as well as death . . . [both involve] sighs, gasps, groans, screams, and rattles concomitant to the described actions . . . Both types of fantasy are completely unrealistic, since they ignore all physical, social, or legal limitations, and both types have complete hallucination of the reader or viewer as their object.[4]

Sociologically, then, it seems that sex and death are often intermingled and reinforcing obsessions. But why is this the case? It may be, as we have asserted, that sex functions as an animal reminder. As

3. Ariès, *Western Attitudes*, 56–57.
4. Gorer, *Death, Grief, and Mourning*, 197–98.

a biological activity sex is a universal aspect of the animal kingdom. We both recognize this fact and are scandalized by it. For example, how many parents have been embarrassed when their children encounter two animals caught in the act of reproduction at the zoo? The scene seems indecent to watch. But these are just animals, right? We are observing a natural biological activity. Nothing pornographic about it, correct? But we stand, embarrassed, and quickly try to move the kids on to the next exhibit.

But the biological, animal function of sex isn't all there is to human sexuality. For humans, sex can be experienced as a deeply *spiritual* activity. Sex is often an experience of spiritual exultation and transcendence. Further, the deepest feelings of human love and union are often experienced within the sex act.

In short, sex is *dual*. Some aspects of sex, as we observe at the zoo, are reminders of our connection with the animals. We even speak of "animialistic sex" or refer to sexual positions as "doggy style." And yet, these animal reminders are connected with an act intimately associated with love and spiritual transcendence. In all this, sex brings us back to Luther's privy: the scandal of anality, the union of the sacred and the profane, the divine linked to the animal.[5]

In sum, sex is no simple death reminder. The dual nature of sex implies that some aspects of sex are elevating while others are degrading and disgusting. Sex is existentially complicated.

An illuminating laboratory study conducted by Jamie Goldenberg, Tom Pyszcynski, Shannon McCoy, Jeff Greenburg, and Sheldon Solomon has explored the existential complications of sex.[6] Specifically, in the study conducted by these researchers participants were initially separated into one of two imagery groups. The first group was asked to imagine the spiritual/romantic aspects of sexual intercourse (e.g., being loved by the partner, connecting spiritually with the partner). Again, these are the aspects of sex that do not function as animal reminders. These are the aspects of sex, like human tears, that are *spiritual* and, thus, high on the divinity dimension, closer to heaven. In contrast, the second group was asked to imagine the physical/bodily

5. Goldenberg et al., "Understanding Human Ambivalence about Sex," 310–20.

6. Goldenberg et al., "Why is Sex Such a Problem?," 1173–87.

aspects of the sexual encounter (e.g., tasting bodily fluids, skin rubbing). These are the animal reminders of sex, the aspects of sex closely associated with the body. These animal-reminder stimuli, being lower on the divinity dimension, can trigger feelings of disgust or degradation. The research question was: are these animal-reminder aspects of sex associated with death/mortality concerns?

After the initial imagery exercise (spiritual versus bodily sex) the two groups were asked to engage in a word-fragment completion task where the word-fragments (e.g., sk_ll, coff _ _) could be completed in either a death (e.g., skull, coffin) or non-death (e.g., skill, coffee) related manner. The results indicated that thinking about the physical/bodily aspects of sex created greater death-thought accessibility (i.e., those in the body imagery condition were significantly more likely to complete the words as *skull* or *coffin* than as *skill* or *coffee*). In short, the physical, animal-reminder aspects of sex did function as mortality-awareness triggers. And these are, as we noted earlier, the same stimuli that make sex revolting, disgusting, or animalistic.

Let's pause and soak this in a bit. The Goldenburg et al. study suggests that Christian attitudes concerning sex cannot be simplistically attributed to the puritanical impulses within certain religious populations. Something more might be going on. Specifically, sex can be *existentially* worrisome. Sex can remind us of our bodies and their associated needs and vulnerabilities. Sex isn't just "wrong": there is something "unclean" and often disgusting about the activity. Sex isn't just "naughty," it can also be "dirty." And one potential for degradation that is inherent in sex is the fact that this spiritually transcendent activity is scandalously linked with a bodily function shared with brute animals. The connection—soul and spirit with semen and sweat—is offensive.

4.

The dynamics surrounding attitudes toward sex are very similar to the dynamics surrounding obscene language. This is not surprising in that obscene language, as Carlin noted, is often centered on the body. Take, for example, the paradigmatic inventory of profanity: George Carlin's famous list of "The Seven Words You Can Never Say on Television." Commenting on Carlin's list, the psychologist Steven Pinker in his book *The Stuff of Thought* has noted the following:

> The seven words you can never say on television refer to sexuality and excretion: they are names for feces, urine, intercourse, the vagina, breasts, a person who engages in fellatio, and a person who acts out an Oedipal desire.[7]

But it's not only sexuality and excretion that are implicated in profanity. Pinker goes on:

> But the capital crime in the Ten Commandments comes from a different subject, theology, and the taboo words in many languages refer to perdition, deities, messiahs, and their associated relics and body parts. Another semantic field that spawns taboo words across the world's languages is death and disease, and still another is disfavored classes of people such as infidels, enemies, and subordinate ethnic groups. But what could these concepts—from mammaries to messiahs to maladies to minorities—possibly have in common?[8]

Pinker suggests that these semantic clusters can be united by noting that profanity generally creates a strong negative emotion. More specifically, many profanities appear to be associated with the psychology of disgust and contamination. Urine, feces, blood, and other bodily effluvia are routinely referenced in obscene speech as well as being reliable disgust elicitors. But the profanity/disgust link is incomplete as it fails to capture facets of religious cursing (e.g., damn, hell), references to sexual intercourse (e.g., the f-word), or references to body parts (e.g., breasts, genitalia). What can link these sources of profanity?

Our existential analysis provides one answer. Profanity might function as a morality reminder. As we observed in the case of sex, mortality concerns are implicated in animal-reminder and body references. This would explain why references to sex, genitalia, and other scatological references are offensive. In a similar way, religious cursing (e.g., "Damn you!," "You can go to hell!") also functions as a death reminder (e.g., a reference to the Judgment after death).

To understand the logic of this conclusion, notice how the f-word functions as a body/animal reference. The f-word exploits the

7. Pinker, *Stuff of Thought*, 326–27.
8. Ibid.

fissure between the physical and the spiritual aspects of sex. Again, sex should be a *dual* act, a *union* of both the physical and the spiritual. Stripped of its spiritual significance and meaning, sex is reduced to its animal function. This is the f-word's power. It strips sex of its spiritual significance, reducing the act to physical manipulations. It short, the f-word functions, literally, as a profanity: something that is considered to be sacred and high on the divinity dimension is stripped of its spiritual content and rendered *profane*.

(This is not to say that the f-word cannot be playfully exploited by sexual partners. Saying *"Let's f***"* in contrast to *"Let's make love"* is a request for a sexual encounter that is more physical than sentimental. The f-word is *picking out the body*, as opposed to the spirit, as the locus of pleasure. "Dirty" sex can be enjoyed in a healthy, loving, and spiritual union. But the illicit nature of this "dirty sex" is mitigated by the spiritual bond shared by the partners. That is, "dirty sex," although highlighting physical pleasure and erotic abandon, remains *dual*, a physical *and* spiritual act. It is a way to indulge the body without moving into degradation, spiritually speaking.)

The links between anality, animals, divinity, and degradation are clearly seen in how we describe taboo language. For example, the word "vulgarity" has its origin in the word *vulgar*, rooted in the historical attempt of social elites to distinguish their speech and habits from the lower, poorer classes. As with profanity, vulgarity is speech that takes something that is lofty and civilized and renders it as base and common. Profanity and vulgarity are "gutter," "bathroom," or "barnyard" speech. It is "low" speech and, thus, given how we understand the divinity dimension (High = Good and Low = Bad), speech that is immoral, sinful, improper, filthy, and dirty.

So it seems clear that profanity and vulgarity are associated with animals ("barnyard speech"), degradation ("gutter speech"), and the scandal of anality ("bathroom speech"). But does profanity function, as we observed in the case of sex, as a *mortality* reminder? Even if the f-word picks out the body and banishes the spirit, does the f-word remind us of *death*?

A recent study of mine is suggestive in this regard.[9] Specifically, in this study I had Christian participants complete measures of

9. Beck, "Profanity," 294–303.

orthodox Christian belief, animal-reminder disgust, and death anxiety. The orthodoxy measure asked the participants to report the degree
to which they believed core Christian doctrine (e.g., "I believe Jesus
is the Divine Son of God."). The disgust measure asked participants
to rate their disgust regarding the animal-reminder disgust stimuli
noted by Paul Rozin and his colleagues (e.g., disgust in response to
gore, deformity, corpses). The death-anxiety measure assessed how
anxious a person feels in contemplating his or her death (e.g., "I am
very much afraid to die.").

After completing these measures the participants were asked to
consider the words *shit, piss,* and *fuck,* rating how offended they become when they hear someone using these words in everyday conversation. These ratings were summed to create a total score for profanity
offense.

The findings were consistent with the notion that profanity, like
sex, has an existential component. First, orthodoxy ratings were unrelated to offense at profanity usage. The trends observed in the study
did not appear to be due to differences in the sentiments between
liberal or conservative Christians. However, both animal-reminder
disgust ratings and death anxiety ratings were associated with profanity offense. Participants most disgusted by the animal-reminder
stimuli reported being the most offended by profanity. Similarly,
participants reporting the most death anxiety were also the most
offended by profanity. Although not conclusive, the results of this
study are consistent with the notion that profanity can function as a
mortality reminder. Profanity can create an existential confrontation,
in essence saying: "You are a reproducing and metabolic animal!" By
highlighting the oozy and disgusting aspects of our bodies profanity
points out our animal nature, mocking any spiritual fantasies that we
might escape, avoid, or minimize our physical existence. Profanity is
a shock to a creature aspiring to be like the angels.

5.

What can we take away from all this?

The point is not to suggest that taboos surrounding sex and
language should be dismantled or rejected. Our analysis here isn't

about normative issues. The goal in analyzing our reactions to sex and taboo language is to probe deeper into the psychology of degradation and disgust. What we find, following Carlin, is that what is often considered to be taboo, illicit, vulgar, indecent, profane, degrading, disgusting, or obscene frequently clusters around worries associated with the body. More specifically, the vulgar and profane tend to cluster around aspects of physical existence that remind us of our physical vulnerabilities, dependencies, and death. In short, the emotions of disgust and degradation are often repressing or hiding deep existential anxieties. Disgust fends off and pushes death anxiety out of consciousness. The worry in all this, as I have suggested and will elaborate in more detail in the next chapter, is that this existential repression and denial is undermining the Christian mission in the world. Existentially motivated disgust is causing the Christian community to *evacuate* the world in the pursuit of "spirituality," "holiness," and "purity." But this escape, this flight from the "brass tacks" of human existence, is, at root, a form of *denial*. Worryingly, due to the unconscious dynamics involved, the church is often unaware that its concerns over purity, dignity, and holiness are actually manifestations of a fear-based defensive response. Such a church, handicapped by its fears and lack of self-awareness, is ill-prepared to move into missional living and a passionate engagement with the world in all its squalor.

In contrast to this fear-based escape from the physical world, the Incarnation itself becomes the model of missionality. Rather than a Gnostic escape into the spiritual, God enters the degradation of physical existence. And yet, given what we have learned about the existential worries implicated in the body, it is not surprising to find that many churches flee, often unwittingly, the body of Jesus. The Incarnation remains a scandal for many. Could this scandal be *existential* in nature? If it is, we discover another location (another theological sweet tooth!) where psychological dynamics are affecting theological reflection and, thus, the mission of the church.

11

Need and Incarnation

And the Word became flesh . . .

—John 1:14

1.

In 1987 the photographer Andres Serrano unveiled his controversial work *Piss Christ*. *Piss Christ* was a photograph of a crucifix submerged in a mixture of blood and urine. The work broke into public consciousness in 1989 when members of the US Senate expressed outrage that Serrano had received $15,000 from the American National Endowment for the Arts. Senators called the work "filth," "blasphemous," and "abhorrent." One Senator said, "In naming it, [Serrano] was taunting the American people. He was seeking to create indignation. That is all right for him to be a jerk but let him be a jerk on his own time and with his own resources. Do not dishonor our Lord." Later, in 1997, the National Gallery in Melbourne, Australia, was closed when members of a Christian group attacked and damaged *Piss Christ*.

If Serrano was seeking to shock, offend, or gain notoriety with *Piss Christ* he certainly succeeded. The knee-jerk response of many Christians to *Piss Christ* is revulsion, disgust, and anger. It was deeply offensive to many to see the cross of Jesus, the most sacred symbol within the Christian faith, submerged in fluids—urine and blood—

that we find disgusting. The contact between Christ and urine is transgressive, degrading, and vile.

Or is it? The Christian response to *Piss Christ* has, actually, been a bit more complex. Far and away, the main responses have been outrage and disgust. But some Christian thinkers have paused in the face of *Piss Christ* and have walked away with a very different set of reactions. Take, as one example, the analysis of Beth Williamson in her book *Christian Art: A Very Short Introduction*. Williamson's analysis is worth quoting in full:

> What are we to make of this work: what are we to understand by it, and how can we interpret it? Most obviously were enraged by the combination of the most iconic image of Christianity—the Crucified Christ—with human bodily fluid, and felt that this work set out deliberately to provoke viewers to outrage. The artist almost certainly aimed to provoke a reaction, but what reaction? The fact that urine is involved is crucial here. But was the use of urine simply intended, as some of Serrano's detractors have claimed, to cause offense? Had the artist deliberately set out to show disrespect to this religious image, by placing it in urine? Some felt this was tantamount to urinating on the crucifix. I would suggest that, even if some viewers and commentators feel that it was the artist's intention, or part of his intention, to be offensive, there are also other ways to interpret this work. Let us acknowledge that if Serrano had only used blood here this image might not have caused such huge outrage. It is, after all, much more common to associate Christ and his body with blood, because of his shedding of blood on the cross. We are used to seeing crucifixes running with blood, and the wounds of Christ spurting blood. While blood may be a bodily fluid that can cause unease, it is not reviled in the same way as a bodily waste product such as urine. The use of the slang or offensive word "piss" in the title of Serrano's work reminds us that this fluid is wholly undesirable. The artist plays upon the viewer's discomfort, even outrage, at seeing the image of Christ crucified, suspended in a mixture of blood and urine, and almost certainly intends to shock, but to what end? I would suggest that the use of urine here is intended to introduce, or in fact restore, some shock to the image of the Crucifixion. After seeing countless reproductions of hundreds of years' worth of Crucifixion images, a modern viewer's reactions to the Crucifixion of Christ might become dulled. A shock such as the one provided by Serrano's *Piss Christ* might remind

a modern viewer what the image of the Crucified Christ really means. The process of viewing the Crucified Christ through the filter of human bodily fluids requires the observer to consider all the ways in which Christ, as both fully divine and fully human, really shared in the base physicality of human beings. As a real human being Christ took on all the characteristics of the human body, including its fluids and secretions. The use of urine here can therefore force the viewer to rethink what it meant for Christ to be really and fully human.[1]

It is very unlikely that Serrano had Williamson's take in mind when he photographed *Piss Christ*. But the intentions of the artist are not available to us. Regardless, each of us is free to interact with the piece as we choose, walking away with interpretations unique to our own perspective. In short, even if Serrano intended *Piss Christ* to be a subversive commentary upon Christianity, I think it perfectly appropriate to use the gospel to read *Piss Christ* subversively, robbing the artwork of its transgressive goal (if that was its intent) and harnessing the shock of the piece as a deep theological commentary regarding the Incarnation.

Let us follow, then, Williamson's suggestion that *Piss Christ* reveals something shocking, illicit, and disgusting about the Incarnation. The connection between Christ and bodily fluids is experienced as offensive, not only in this artwork but also in our imaginations. Many Christians throughout history have resisted the notion of the Incarnation, that Jesus was physically vulnerable, experienced erections, vomited when ill, or experienced diarrhea. Connecting Jesus with the body has always seemed blasphemous and degrading. It is Luther's privy all over again, the offensive combination of the spiritual with the disgustingly physical. The title of Serrano's work—*Piss Christ*—vividly demonstrates our offense at the *connection*. The two worlds, the life of the body and the life of Christ, should be separated.

In my own research I've called this squeamishness *Incarnational ambivalence*: the worry, denial, or offense at a fully human Jesus. We often see Incarnational ambivalence on display when outrage is directed toward robust depictions of the humanity of Jesus. One example was the Christian outrage and protests surrounding the Martin

1. Williamson, *Christian Art*, 114–16.

Scorsese film *The Last Temptation of Christ* based upon the novel by Nikos Kazantzakis. In the film Jesus is tempted on the cross (the last temptation he faces) to come down off the cross to pursue a normal human life, full of the joys of marriage and family life. In picturing this temptation, Jesus is shown marrying Mary Magdalene, which is followed by a scene of the married couple making love. This scene— Jesus engaging in sex—was a locus of Christian outrage. The tacit admission of this outrage is that Jesus would never have been tempted by sexual desire and that the life of the body held no appeal to him.

2.

Incarnational ambivalence is not a new or recent phenomenon. Throughout Christian history believers have resisted the notion of the Incarnation. A central doctrinal debate of the early church centered on the humanity of Jesus. Was Jesus both *fully* divine and *fully* human? Theology aside, the psychological tensions here are, as we've seen, almost unbearable. Consequently, there are strong pressures to resolve the tension in one way or the other. For example, the Gnostics and Docetists leaned one way, seeking to deny Jesus full participation in the human condition. Leaning the other way were the followers of Arius who, in light of Jesus' physical body, denied the fully pre-existent divinity of Christ. The early church eventually navigated between these two views, strongly asserting both the full humanity and the full divinity of Christ. But this view is full of psychological tensions, tensions still very much with us. The union of the spiritual and physical has always been problematic.

But why is the notion of a fully human Jesus so scandalous? We have in hand some psychological answers to this question, but it might also be helpful to approach the question historically, to see if we might find a theological convergence upon our psychological analysis. So let's ask, what were the concerns of Arius and his followers? What where they trying to accomplish in denying the pre-existent divinity of Jesus?

Arthur C. McGill in his book *Suffering: A Test of Theological Method* describes the goals of Arius in his debates with Athanasius re-

garding the divinity of Jesus. Specifically, according to McGill, Arius
was trying to uphold the honor of God:

> In all the history of Christianity there has hardly been so so-
> phisticated, so Biblically grounded, and so thoroughgoing a
> theology of God's transcendence as developed by Arius and his
> followers. Their whole concern was to honor God by setting
> him above and in contrast to his creatures. They sought to pre-
> serve the glory of God by divesting his reality of all those weak-
> nesses and deficiencies which mark his creatures, and by giving
> him the most absolute kind of mastery over his creatures.[2]

Wanting to protect the absolute Otherness of God, a worthy
goal, Arius and his followers insisted that any physical, created ("be-
gotten") thing could not, by definition, fully partake of the divine
nature. The debates surrounding the doctrine of the Trinity, therefore, were not about the paradoxes of the math (i.e., how can God
be Three in One?). Rather, admission of Jesus into the Trinity was a
debate about the *qualities* and *nature* of God. McGill summarizes:

> The issue between Arius and Athanasius, then, has nothing to
> do with whether God is one or two or three. It has to do with
> what quality makes God divine, what quality constitutes his
> perfection. From the perspective of self-contained absolute-
> ness and transcendent supremacy, Arius can only look upon
> God's begetting a Son as a grotesque blasphemy.[3]

The problem with Arius' view of God, according to Athanasius,
is that Arius' self-contained and perfect God is *sterile*. Arius' God
needs nothing. Consequently, Arius' God cannot love. Love, according to McGill, presupposes *need*. The Son *needs* the Father and the
Father, to be love, *needs* the Son. By placing need and dependency
(the Son) within the Godhead, the dynamic, mutual, and self-giving
nature of love is now found to characterize the life of God. Love, via
the need of the Son, is deified in the interactions of the Trinity. As
McGill summarizes, "Love and not transcendence, giving and not being superior, are the qualities that mark God's divinity." Thus, "since

2. McGill, *Suffering*, 72–73.
3. Ibid., 78.

giving entails receiving, there must be a receptive, dependent pole within the being of God."[4]

Why is the Incarnation so shocking? Why do we resist the notion of a fully human Jesus? Following McGill, it appears that we are deeply ambivalent about our *neediness*. We feel that our neediness, our physical vulnerabilities and dependencies, are disgusting, degrading, and offensive. And nothing signifies this neediness more strongly than the human body. Feeling this degradation we seek to protect God from need, to create quarantines around God. God, thus, is self-contained, perfect, and holy. But inherent in this impulse is *a flight from our own need*, a refusal to exist in a state of need. The Church Fathers have always claimed that the primal human sin is the desire to become "God-like." We often think about this desire as some sort of "pride." This is true, but it is a conceit of a particular sort. Specifically, we posit a self-contained God, a God that needs nothing. And with this as the *Imago Dei, we then seek to become like this God,* self-contained and self-sufficient, needing nothing to sustain ourselves. In short, *a denial of the Incarnation is an attempt to flee from our need* and, as we will see, this undermines our capacity to love. Here is McGill once again:

> It is very common for men within the satanic frame of reference to identify need as the great "flaw" in things. Therefore, they picture God as one who lacks this flaw, who has no needs, who stands independently and immutably within the circle of his own identity. What they feel compelled to remove from their picture of God is that which they most fear and most despair; their own condition of need.[5]

Is this analysis correct? Is our ambivalence concerning the Incarnation a flight from our own need, dependency, and vulnerability? Our discussions over the last few chapters seem to answer in the affirmative. Our utter dependency is nowhere more manifest than in our vulnerability to death. In fact, *death is what defines human need*. The forces of death are always at work in my body. And to fend off death, I must *eat* and *excrete*. I am always moving into hunger, always in *need*. And if I eat, I must defecate and urinate. The whole

4. Ibid., 78.
5. Ibid., 99–100.

metabolic cycle is driven by the forces of death and decay and my daily efforts to fend them off.

In short, as we have been discussing over the last two chapters, our feelings of disgust, revulsion, and offense at the body are often rooted in mortality fears. Our squeamishness concerning the Incarnation is driven by an impulse to deny our need, to deny the role of death in our lives. A latent death anxiety sits behind our reactions to *Piss Christ*.

3.

Is there any evidence that death anxiety is implicated in Incarnational ambivalence? A recent study of mine is illuminating on this point.

It seems clear, given our review of the psychological research, that the body functions as a death reminder. Thus, it is reasonable to expect that the people most fearful of death would be the most resistant to Incarnational images. That is, people reporting greater death anxiety should be the most offended by images of Jesus' physical and metabolic neediness and dependency. In a recent study, I examined this association.[6] Specifically, I asked Christian participants to complete measures, among others, of death anxiety and Incarnational ambivalence to examine the relationship between the two variables.

The Incarnational ambivalence measure was created to assess four broad body scenarios that had been shown in previous research to function as death/mortality reminders: body fluids, body flaws, hygiene, and physical vulnerability. Respondents were asked to read examples of various body scenarios under each category and to imagine Jesus experiencing (or affected by) that particular physical condition. Under the category of *body fluids* there were three scenarios: diarrhea, nocturnal emissions, and vomit. Under the *body flaws* category there were four scenarios: scarring (due to a childhood illness), tooth decay, near-sightedness, and malformation (due to a birth defect). Under the *hygiene* category there were three scenarios: bad breath, body odor, and dandruff. Finally, under the *physical vulnerability* category there were two scenarios: chronic back pain and chronic headaches.

6. Beck, "Feeling Queasy about the Incarnation," 303–12.

After imagining Jesus in each scenario respondents were asked to give their reactions across four dimensions. These were:

1. This image makes me uncomfortable.
2. This image is demeaning to Jesus.
3. This image is unrealistic.
4. This image is unbiblical.

The first two prompts were created to capture an *emotional* response to the scenario (i.e., discomfort, offense) while the last two prompts were drafted to capture a more *intellectual*, perhaps theological, response. All four ratings ended up being highly correlated. That is, individuals who found a particular image demeaning were also likely to report the image as uncomfortable, unbliblical, and unrealistic. The measure of Incarnational ambivalence was the sum of the four ratings across all the body scenarios.

And as predicted, death anxiety was positively correlated with Incarnational ambivalence. The participants most fearful of death were the ones most likely to reject the body scenarios. Those participants less fearful of death were more comfortable with the images.

This result, tentative as it is, appears to support the notion that our offense at the Incarnation is (at least partly) driven by a denial of our own neediness, particularly as those needs cluster around the recognition of our own mortality. Death is the great demonstration of our need. Thus, the body, as the constant witness of both our need and death, is experienced as disgusting and degrading. For us, and for Jesus.

4.

All this discussion concerning the body, sex, offensive artwork, excrement, profanity, and the Incarnation might be very interesting, but what does it have to do with the life and mission of the church? Do our mortality fears, which cluster around the body, affect our capacity to live lives of welcome, inclusion, and embrace? And how, exactly, does body ambivalence connect with the events in Matthew 9? How does any of this relate to the notion of "God desires mercy, not sacrifice"?

In the gospel of Matthew the refrain from Hosea—"I desire mercy, not sacrifice"—occurs on two different occasions. The first, as we have been discussing, occurs in Matthew 9 in the context of table fellowship. In Matthew 9 Jesus attacks notions of purity ("sacrifice") that trump the "will to embrace." But there seems to be little in Matthew 9 that speaks to the feelings of body ambivalence that we have been discussing here in Part 4.

The second occurrence of "I desire mercy, not sacrifice" occurs in Matthew 12. Interestingly, the events in Matthew 12 have nothing to do with issues of table fellowship and hospitality. But the events of Matthew 12 do circle around the body and its physical dependencies, needs, and vulnerabilities. The triggering event in the narrative is *hunger*. Jesus' disciples pick grain to eat on the Sabbath, violating the injunctions to refrain from work. As a result, the disciples become ritually "unclean." In the face of this critique from the Pharisees Jesus recalls another story of hunger trumping the purity codes. Jesus reminds the Pharisees that David and his men once ate the temple bread when they were desperately hungry. Having pointed out this story, Jesus cites, for the second time in Matthew, the refrain that God "desires mercy, not sacrifice." This exchange is quickly followed by another conflict with the Pharisees. This second confrontation concerns healing a man with a withered hand on the Sabbath. Is it lawful to heal this man on the Sabbath? Jesus defends the healing he is about to perform by asking the Pharisees if they would rescue a sheep they owned if it had fallen into a ditch on the Sabbath. The sheep was, obviously, in that time and place, a source of family food and income. The sheep is an *economic* illustration (today Jesus might have said: "Imagine if you dropped your paycheck in a ditch. Wouldn't you go in after it?"). So, yes, of course the Pharisees would pull the sheep from the ditch. Their ability to feed themselves demands the action. The Pharisees, just like the disciples and David, need to eat.

What we find in Matthew 12 is less a conflict over hospitality than a debate over the recognition of human biological need. Human need and biological vulnerability fill Matthew 12. The issues swirl around hunger, an animal in a ditch, and a deformed hand. Each of these, as we have seen here in Part 4, is a disgust trigger. Animals, metabolic functions, and physical malformation are all disgust stimuli. And we are also now positioned to note that these stimuli are often disgusting because they remind us of human need, vulnerability, and, ultimately, death. Consequently, it is very interesting to observe how Jesus connects, with the refrain of "I desire mercy, not sacrifice," this recognition of human need with his own ministry of table fellowship. Mercy, for Jesus, seems to be deeper than mere social affiliation and contact. For Jesus, mercy is implicated in *the recognition of human neediness*. As seen in Matthew 12, humans go hungry and our ability to meet our basic biological needs can become catastrophically compromised (e.g., when a farm animal falls in a ditch, you are without food, or a physical disability impairing your ability to work). In short, the problem with the Pharisees was not just their unwillingness to *associate* with the "unclean." The Pharisees were also blinded to signs of human *need*. This seems to be due to the fact that the Pharisees were blind to their *own* need. The Pharisees do not notice their economic and biological vulnerability until Jesus points out that they would quickly pull their sheep from a ditch, even if it was on the Sabbath. The Pharisees could not see how needy they were, how vulnerable they were as biological creatures. And by denying this about themselves the Pharisees could not see need in others, damning the hungry disciples when they fed themselves or refusing healing to a man with a useless hand. By pointing out how quickly life can change, biologically and economically, Jesus forces the Pharisees to confront their own vulnerability in the hope that a "will to embrace" might become kindled within their hearts.

In summary, what we see in Matthew 12 is how a flight into purity is often a flight *from the body* into the divine. More precisely, the flight into purity is often a flight from *need* into *self-sufficiency*. And this flight into purity and self-sufficiency has catastrophic effects upon human compassion and empathy (what Jesus calls "mercy"). The delusional desire to deny the body and flee the Incarnation might simply be a psychological curiosity if it were not for the fact that the pursuit of self-sufficiency makes the church insensitive and unresponsive in the face of human vulnerability, weakness, and suffering.

5.

But embracing our vulnerability is extraordinarily difficult. As we have noted, the denial of death is, inherently, a denial of our neediness. Disgust pushes away all reminders of our biological need, contingency, vulnerability, and dependency.

This repression of death and need is particularly acute in America and other modern, technologically advanced nations. The reason for this is that our material wealth and technological success obscure our need and vulnerability. Never suffering want or poverty, and trusting in modern medicine, Americans can live (and pretend) as if they were immortal. This creates a cultural worldview that is characterized by what Ernest Becker has called "the denial of death," the refusal to admit the reality of death into our lives and consciousness. Arthur C. McGill gives another cogent analysis of this in his description of American death repression in his book *Death and Life: An American Theology*. In *Death and Life* McGill notes that "Americans like to appear as if they give death hardly any thought at all."[7] The American ethic is, thus, "for people to create a living world where death seems abnormal and accidental. [Americans] must create a living world where life is so full, so secure, and so rich with possibilities that it gives no hint of death and deprivation."[8]

What we see in this death repression is a *collective* and *cultural* denial of our own vulnerability and need. The American duty, according to McGill, is to be "fine," to take up "the duty to look well, to seem fine, to exclude from the fabric of [our] normal life any evidence of decay and death and helplessness."[9] This social pressure to be "fine," to hide from others our vulnerability and failure, is the dark and pathological side of the American success ethos. It is the drive to become so materially successful as to eliminate all trace of need. It is the quest, as noted above, to be god-like: separate, autonomous, self-contained, and without need.

7. McGill, *Death and Life*, 13.
8. Ibid., 18.
9. Ibid., 19–20.

Aspiring to be god-like, Americans live with "the conviction that the lives we live are not essentially and intrinsically mortal."[10] But this, says McGill, this is a "dream," an "illusory realm of success."[11] "Refusing to be lacerated by the horrors of life, [Americans] create [a] world of life-affirming buoyancy."[12] Americans accomplish this illusion by devoting themselves "to expunging from their lives every appearance, every intimation of death . . . All traces of weakness, debility, ugliness and helplessness must be kept away from every part of a person's life. The task must be done every single day if such persons really are to convince us that they do not carry the smell of death within them."[13] As we have seen, disgust aids in this death repression. Feeling revulsion and contempt in the face of physical failure and decay, in both ourselves and others, we push death and need out of consciousness.

But so what? Why is it so important to recognize our need and mortality? Why dwell on these morbid topics? Why face death and decay?

There are many answers to these questions. For example, many cultures and faiths have recognized the spiritual benefits found in squarely confronting death. Humans can waste life, acting as if time were a replenishable and inexhaustible resource. We live, practically speaking, as if we were immortal and god-like, as if we had "all the time in the world." Consequently, many religious traditions encourage meditation on morbid subjects. The goal is to recognize the transitory nature and the preciousness of life so that we live deeply and don't "waste" life.

Recognizing the gift of life and puncturing delusional aspirations toward immortality are certainly worthy goals. But these are not, for our purposes, the most important reasons the church needs to confront death and human need. The real reason the church must fight against death repression is the reason we observed in Matthew 12: honestly embracing need is critical for a life of mercy.

10. Ibid., 27.
11. Ibid., 35.
12. Ibid., 37.
13. Ibid., 26.

As we observed with the Pharisees, blindness to our need also blinds us to the need in others. It is a matter of empathy, compassion, and solidarity. Never experiencing poverty, we fail to understand why the poor ("those people on welfare") just don't go out and get a job. Our smug, self-contained, god-like success creates gaps of understanding and compassion. And, once again, we find disgust creating boundaries between people. In this case disgust at the poor hides our own vulnerabilities, allowing us to pretend we are gods, self-determined agents. From this Olympian vantage point, we cannot empathize with the teeming unwashed masses below us. Recall the events in the Corinthian church where the wealthy Christians, secure in their material existence, ate and drank to excess, never realizing that their poorer brothers and sisters were going hungry in the outer rooms of the house. Blind to their own need, the affluent Christians in Corinth could not see the need in others.

But this goes deeper than empathy. As hinted at in our discussion of the Trinity, love is not possible without need. As the Church Fathers asserted, a self-contained God without need is sterile. For God to be love there has to be a Son, a needy, receiving component within the Godhead. God the Father empties himself into the Son and the Son returns that glory to the Father. The love, nature, and life of God are revealed in this dynamic cycle of *emptying* and *receiving* between Father and Son.

And so it is for Christians seeking to step into the life and love of God. Christian love cannot be from our *excess*. Love is not letting go of the leftovers, the margin left behind after we have taken care of our material needs and secured our creature comforts. Recall how Jesus praises the widow at the temple who gave two pennies because it was "all she owned." Alongside this widow the wealthy gave from their excess. The contrast, for Jesus, concerns self-giving to the point of neediness. The widow, giving all she had, *moves into a state of need* with her gift. The wealthy give a greater sum but remain self-sustaining and self-determined. McGill's powerful analysis on this point is worth quoting at length:

> The love which is proclaimed in many churches that worship the [American] dream carefully disregards the outcome of love. These churches speak of love as helping others, but they ignore

what helping others does to the person who loves. They ignore the fact that love is self-expenditure, a real expending, a real losing, a real deterioration of the self. They speak as if the person who is loving had no problems, had no needs . . . They say to people: "Since you have no unanswered needs, why don't you go and help the other people who are in need?" But they never go on to add "If you do this, you too will be driven into need." By not stating the outcome of love they give the childish impression that Christian love is some kind of cornucopia where we can meet everyone's needs and problems and still have everything we need for ourselves! And believe me, there are grown-up people who speak this kind of nonsense . . . [all this is the] illusion that some people can give without receiving, can nourish others without thereby becoming impoverished themselves—in short the illusion of perpetual affluence . . . the dreadfulness of this illusion lies in the fact that it is so inauthentic; it is so phony . . . If ever you approach a needy person with the illusion that you are a creature of purely bestowing love, then to that needy person you will seem totally alien, totally superior . . . Active love occurs within the fellowship of neediness, within the neediness of the one who serves and leads, and the one who serves in neediness . . . Too often we hear the lie that to love is to help others without this help having any effect upon ourselves.[14]

This is the deep reason as to why blindness to our own need undermines a life of mercy. The issue does begin with *empathy*, seeing my need reflected in the lives of others. But it doesn't stop there. Mercy is *costly*. True love *moves me into need*. Which is, admittedly, a scary prospect. It is an act of faith and it requires a *community*, a "fellowship of neediness" to use McGill's phrase. And it is within the giving and receiving of this "fellowship of neediness" where the life and love of God is fully expressed and experienced. In this, the life of the Trinity creates the life of the church or, rather, the life of the church participates in the life of the triune God.

But none of this can happen if disgust continues to foster a "denial of death" by pushing away all reminders of decay and biological need. Once again we see the need to dismantle disgust psychology if we are to move into experiences we perceive as morbid, demeaning, and disgusting. Disgust and contempt prevent us from recognizing

14. Ibid., 87–88, 89, 90.

and embracing the need, vulnerability, death, and decay within our own lives. Because, despite appearances and protestations to the contrary, we are not "fine." And by admitting as much we embrace, without disgust or distain, our fragile and shared humanity. We embrace neediness as the only route available to us if we are to be a people of grace, mercy, and love.

Conclusion

Elimination and Regulation

Take and eat . . .

—**Matt 26:26**

1.

Throughout this book I have made a sustained argument that the psychology of disgust is at work in the life of the church. Disgust and the attributions of contamination affect how we reason about morality, our experience of grace, and our relationship to the holy. Disgust also affects how we experience otherness, placing keen pressures upon the Christian call to hospitality. Finally, disgust is implicated in ambivalence about our neediness and vulnerability, prompting a Gnostic flight from the "brass tacks" of human existence.

In each of these cases we have observed how the psychology of disgust functions as a theological "sweet tooth," pulling normative and theological reflection into orbits that are unhealthy and often contrary to the Christian mission. For example, humans, it appears, seem to reason about morality in the idiom of cleanliness. As a mere metaphor this is not problematic. But laboratory tests examining the Macbeth Effect have shown how easy it is, due to the close association between morality and cleanliness, for physical cleansing to replace moral effort. What we see in this is how a psychological dynamic is tempting the church into a religious-based cleansing that might have little to nothing to do with passionate missional engagement with the world. Such a church "feels" clean to itself, but its engagement with the world remains insipid and static. The Macbeth Effect is, at root, the concern Jesus has about the Pharisees in the gospel of Matthew:

> Woe to you, teachers of the law and Pharisees, you hypocrites! You clean the outside of the cup and dish, but inside they are full of greed and self-indulgence. Blind Pharisee! First clean the inside of the cup and dish, and then the outside also will be clean.

Beyond moral performance we've seen how disgust affects theological reflection. For example, Christians throughout the centuries have struggled with the scandal of the Incarnation, Jesus' full participation in the human condition. There is something illicit and vulgar about imagining Jesus participating in the metabolic life of the body, or pulled by the sexual desires associated with human reproduction. Consequently, at various times and places throughout Christian history, there have been attempts to quarantine Jesus from the life of the body, to embrace a *super*-human Jesus. We've discovered that this flight from the body of Jesus is partly driven by the existential aspects of disgust, how disgust protects us from reminders of our physical need and vulnerability. The worry, obviously, is that this Gnostic view of the Incarnation promotes a spirituality that becomes "too spiritual," a spirituality that becomes otherworldly and radically disconnected from the physical realities of human existence. Such a view of the Incarnation promotes a withdrawal and flight from the world.

Finally, we have also discussed how disgust creates our experience of otherness. More specifically, we observed how disgust and love function, in tension, as a boundary psychology. Consequently, love is impossible if disgust (or associated emotions such as contempt) is operative. This seems obvious when we considered disgust at its genocidal worst, the eradication of monsters and scapegoats. However, psychological research has shown that sociomoral fissures exist in every human heart. For many of us, humanity ends at the borders of our tribes. This is the social psychological dynamic that causes the moral circle to shrink by focusing my acts of giving and kindness on the very few. Thus, if the Christian is to embrace the call to hospitality, the dynamics of otherness must be mastered at a deep psychological level. Miroslav Volf calls this the "will to embrace."

2.

So what are we to do about disgust psychology in the life of the church? It seems clear that disgust psychology produces a variety of noxious outcomes that affect the missional, normative, theological, and social life of the church. Consequently, the church should consciously and intentionally confront disgust psychology to eliminate the worst of its effects. Again, I find the metaphor of the sweet tooth helpful here. Disgust psychology cannot be eliminated from the life of the church. The pull of disgust will remain a constant temptation, pulling the less vigilant, as will our sweet tooth, into overindulgence. The goal for the church is to live life managing this sweet tooth, embracing disgust when it serves a legitimate protective function but rejecting the impulse when it produces social exclusion, a Macbeth Effect-type hypocrisy, or a Gnostic flight from the body. Life with disgust will be, for the church, similar to managing one's diet. Disgust must be managed intentionally, continually, and with mutual accountability.

So how might this look in practice? How can the church manage and regulate the psychology of disgust in its life and experience? To conclude this book, I would like to explore two possible alternatives.

3.

First, it might be argued that disgust psychology is so toxic and immune to reason that we might elect to systematically remove its influence in the life of the church. That is, one way to manage disgust in the life of the church would be to seek its *elimination*, to allow disgust no purchase upon the hearts and minds of the church. There is much to recommend this response. Notions of purity and holiness create judgments regarding pollution, defilement, and contamination. These are dangerous attributions. Purity and holiness carve the world into clean and unclean and then direct feelings of revulsion and contempt toward the self or the other, those designated as "unclean." Once these judgments and boundaries are in place, it is almost impossible to see how the mission of the church can be accomplished. Given all this, it might just be safer to eliminate purity and holiness categories from the life of the church, to restrict or eliminate their use in the faith community. This is not to say that purity and holiness categories are *wrong*, just that the psychology they activate is *socially and morally dangerous* and difficult to tame. Psychologically and socially, purity and holiness are akin to nuclear weapons. The judgments they create tend to be catastrophic. Consequently, purity might be a category the church should just leave alone. It's just too dangerous. People get hurt.

Such a recommendation is similar to the case made by Martha Nussbaum in her book *Hiding from Humanity*. In *Hiding*, Nussbaum, a legal philosopher, asks if disgust can be a reliable guide for law and social policy. On first blush it seems that disgust could be a legitimate part of civic discourse as we negotiate our social contracts. That is, society might seek to regulate certain aspects of social life when behaviors or activities are widely deemed to be profane, obscene, or disgusting. Consequently, the emotion of disgust might be taken as a legitimate warrant in deciding law or policy. Activity X is *illegal* (or in need of regulation) because it is *disgusting*.

But Nussbaum argues that it is problematic to use disgust as a criterion for law. First, as we discussed in Chapter 4, disgust is a dumbfounding emotion. When there is no agreement on what is considered to be profane or illicit, we are at a loss when we try to adjudicate between viewpoints. For example, in the pornography case of Jacobellis v. Ohio (1964), Supreme Court Justice Potter Stewart famously struggled in his opinion to define pornography:

> I shall not today attempt further to define the kinds of material I understand to be embraced within that shorthand description [i.e., pornography]; and perhaps I could never succeed in intelligibly doing so. But I know it when I see it . . .

Nussbaum would argue that an "I know it when I see it" criterion is no basis for important matters of law and public policy. And yet, when issues of propriety, decorum, or illicitness are being debated the "I know it when I see it" criterion is all we can deploy, as Justice

Stewart famously realized. Propriety is a felt experience that has no objective basis; it exists only within the subjective experience of the individual. This makes adjudication on the basis of disgust notoriously vague, fickle, and idiosyncratic. "I know it when I see it" fails miserably when people see things differently. And they often do.

A similar dumbfounding occurs within the church when individuals within the faith community hold differing sensibilities about what is appropriate, offensive, or blasphemous. In short, disgust might prompt a discussion about what is acceptable or unacceptable, but additional criteria are often needed if we are to make any headway. Importantly, these additional criteria need to be publicly available. Usually these will be references to a location of harm or injustice. But if other criteria are available, criteria we can all agree on, why make the appeal to disgust in the first place? Why not reduce legal and policy issues to *objective considerations* of freedom, equality, and harm? This is the crux of Nussbaum's argument. Let's keep disgust out of law and policy. Perhaps a similar recommendation might work for the church.

A second problem with using disgust as a criterion of law and policy is that disgust is a difficult emotion to control. If allowed to regulate social life, disgust can have disastrous consequences. Nussbaum summarizes:

> [Disgust's] propensity for magical thinking and its connection to group-based prejudice and exclusion make it look particularly unreliable . . . even the moralized form of disgust partakes in the demand for purity and freedom from contamination, a demand that is all to easily connected to the denigration of persons who are unpopular, and too little tethered to any concrete issue of wrongdoing, for which evidence might be offered and examined.[1]

In light of these noxious social outcomes Nussbaum rejects disgust as a criterion for the law. While she admits the adaptive and protective functions of disgust, she ultimately concludes that disgust is too toxic a foundation upon which to build a just and civil society.

Again, a similar analysis might apply to church. Disgust, given its socially dangerous and dumbfounding nature, should be margin-

---

1. Nussbaum, *Hiding*, 125.

alized in the life of the church. However, such a move would involve a dramatic reframing of the purity and holiness categories within the biblical witness. In fact, this is exactly what many faith communities have done. Jesus' statement of "I desire mercy, not sacrifice" is read strongly as a rejection of Levitical notions of purity in favor of an ethic of love and mercy. According to this reading, Jesus is deconstructing the purity tradition of the Old Testament by folding purity into mercy. *Injustice* is what makes us *unclean*. The purity language is retained but its inner meaning has been reconfigured.

One way to frame this reading of "I desire mercy, not sacrifice" is to suggest that Jesus is forming *an identity relationship* between the Greatest Commandments, loving God and loving one's neighbor. That is, rather than seeing these commands as separate injunctions that might, at times, compete with each other, the commands are *fused*, forming an identity. Loving God *becomes* loving my neighbor, with no remainder. This identity is most clearly articulated in 1 John 4:20–21:

> If anyone says, "I love God," yet hates his brother, he is a liar.
> For anyone who does not love his brother, whom he has seen,
> cannot love God, whom he has not seen. And he has given us
> this command: Whoever loves God must also love his brother.

The goal of this identity relationship is to keep the Greatest Commandments from being uncoupled and dislocated. As seen in Matthew 9, the pursuit of purity is very often understood to be a way of "loving" or "pleasing" God. As a consequence, my pursuit of purity and holiness—loving God—comes to compromise my ability to love my neighbor. The most tragic form of dislocation between the Greatest Commandments occurs when the pursuit of holiness leads to God-sanctioned violence, killing to *please* God.

So there seem to be some excellent social and moral reasons for conflating the Greatest Commandments. But there are some concerns here as well. Specifically, when the Greatest Commandments form an identity relationship, the vertical, transcendent pursuit of holiness and purity is collapsed into the horizontal, immanent affairs of human relationships. Something is both gained and lost in this collapse. The gain, as we have just noted, is obvious. The pleasing of

God can never become dislocated from the treatment of the other. *Sacrifice* has been folded into *mercy*. Purity is *identified* with justice.

But the cost of this move is the loss of the transcendent dimension. Without this transcendent dimension the Christian life becomes, essentially, a *political* pursuit. Pleasing God becomes the activity of seeking justice and mercy for all of humanity, to work toward the vision of Advent: "Peace on earth, good will to all."

We have, interestingly, already encountered these issues and tensions. Recall the research regarding the moral foundations and the differences between conservatives and liberals in how they deploy those foundations in making normative judgments. Conservatives make appeals to the Purity/Sanctity foundation while liberals restrict their moral judgments to the foundations of Harm/Care and Fairness/Reciprocity. This is simply another way of saying that liberals, weakly or strongly, reject appeals to a vertical, transcendent dimension (i.e., the sacred and holy) in favor of the horizontal/political dimension of human affairs. By contrast, conservatives will contend that there are times when the sacred—agreement with the vertical dimension—should be privileged over the horizontal/human call for justice or equity. Liberals have largely rejected the vertical dimension, folding it into the immanent concerns of justice and equity. For liberals, the metaphysical ("the sacred") isn't a category worthy of consideration if real world harm and injustice are at stake. In the end, for the liberal, only justice and equity count as legitimate moral warrants. And as we have discussed, this disagreement about the legitimacy of the sacred in public life goes a fair way in explaining how liberals and conservatives approach various policy issues. For example, gay marriage is rejected by conservatives in light of a desire to protect the "sanctity" of marriage and to honor religious prohibitions about the practice of homosexuality. Liberals, by contrast, given their tight focus on justice and equity, see the issue as fundamentally one of basic fairness.

4.

This, then, is one path the church could take. Finding disgust psychology too toxic and unmanageable, the church might reframe or eliminate purity categories from its life and practice. This is accomplished by forming an identity relationship between the Greatest Commandments, effectively collapsing the vertical pursuit of holiness into the immanent pursuit of mercy, equity, and justice. We generally describe this as a *liberal* move, where the moral foundation of purity is shelved in favor of the foundations of justice and equity.

In describing this liberal movement I am, in fact, simply describing the rise of liberal humanism and secularism in the West. Broadly speaking, over the last 500 years the West has moved away from a religious worldview to a secular, humanistic worldview. And this change, the advent of the "secular age," provides us with a case study that allows us to explore the gains and losses facing the church if notions of "purity" and "holiness" are eliminated or deconstructed.

As Charles Taylor discusses in his book *A Secular Age*, one of the driving forces behind the rise of secularism was the collapse of the transcendent dimension in human affairs. Much of this collapse was driven by the Protestant Reformation and the dissolution of the clergy/laity distinction. This dissolution had two related effects. First, it moved us toward a disenchanted world. The ancient world was *enchanted*, filled with spirits, ghosts, and sacred mysteries. The church, being set apart from worldly affairs and alive with supernatural power, inhabited this enchanted, mysterious realm. But during the Protestant Reformation the divisions between sacred and profane places, offices, and rituals were dissolved. Protestant churches became functional "meeting places," a disenchanted space in stark contrast to the enchanted medieval cathedral.

A second outcome of the clergy/laity fusion was an increased moral burden upon the laity. In medieval Christianity holiness was an occupation carried out by church professionals: the clergy, the monastic orders, and the saints. The "holiness professionals" built up reserves of merit that could be appealed to, purchased, and generally relied on. These "merit reserves" carried, spiritually speaking, the laity. But with reform, holiness specialists were no longer set apart. Everyone was now "a saint" and each person was expected to carry his or her own moral burden. This moral pressure upon the common person was unprecedented and was a significant force in the rise of secularism. As Taylor writes, with the rise of reform there was "an attempt to make the mass of the laity . . . shape up more fully as Christians."[2] This increased moral burden upon the laity also collapsed the distinction between the town and the church. In light of reform, Taylor writes, "all valid Christian vocations are those of ordinary life, or production and reproduction in the world. The crucial issue is how you live these vocations. The two spheres are collapsed into each other. Monastic rules disappear, but ordinary lay life is now under more stringent demands. Some of the ascetic norms of monastic life are now transferred to the secular."[3]

Why would this moral pressure on the masses produce secularism? Taylor suggests that the moral intensification on the laity (along with disenchantment) made morality the *telos*, the goal of the Christian faith. What we owe God is *goodness*. As a result of disenchanted reform, Christianity became less *spiritual* but more *moral*. Further, while this moral reform was going on there was an increased valuing of mechanistic, instrumental reason (e.g., Newtonian physics). Consequently, in reform we see religious groups applying instrumental, mechanistic reason to solve the problem of morally educating the polis. Reform goes civic. This moral and civic reform, the implementation of a kind of "moral engineering," was most clearly seen in Calvin's Geneva. In effect, the entire city or nation becomes the monastery. Spirituality goes political.

From here, according to Taylor, it was only a short step from these reforming Protestant political experiments to secular humanism. In short, if goodness (or its more public face "civility") is the goal, and if reason alone can be used to create well-functioning moral communities, then God and the sacred becomes less and less important. Reason and nature become guides to the good life, politically understood. God grows more distant, mainly thanked for creating reason and a morally coherent universe. The moral core of this civic and political existence would be for citizens to practice a "universal beneficence" that would foster peace and a well-functioning society. This "universal beneficence" became the hallmark of humanism, the

2. Taylor, *Secular Age*, 265.
3. Ibid., 266.

focus on equality and justice that is the defining moral virtue of secular societies.[4]

Summarizing Taylor's analysis, during the Protestant Reformation
the transcendent dimension was collapsed into the horizontal plane
of human affairs. One outcome of this collapse, the movement from
enchantment to disenchantment, was the humanistic focus on civic
and political life. The affairs of the town, and not the church, were
the most important and in need of reform. With the loss of the sacred, the pursuit of purity and holiness was replaced with political
concern and civic action. The secular age thus finds its life in what
Taylor calls "the immanent frame," the plane of solely human affairs
after the collapse of the sacred.

Generally speaking, liberal churches have followed this path,
pursuing faith in the immanent frame. One positive outcome of this
choice is the marginalization of disgust psychology. With the collapse
of the sacred we see a decline in the pursuit of holiness and purity,
separate from immanent moral or political concerns. But there are
costs to be considered as well. Despite the political focus on justice
and equity, the immanent frame can seem hollow, devoid of meaning, and insipid. As Taylor notes, "There is a generalized sense in our
culture that with the eclipse of the transcendent, something may
have been lost."[5] In the immanent frame, "the quotidian is emptied
of deeper resonance, is dry, flat; the things which surround us are
dead, ugly, empty; and the way we organize them, shape them, in
order to live has not meaning, beauty, depth, sense."[6] In the secular
age, we now experience "a terrible flatness in the everyday."[7]

Following Taylor, we can see the path ahead for a church that
seeks to eliminate disgust psychology from its life and practice. Such
a church would follow the liberalizing impulse, folding the transcendent into the immanent. Such a church would define its ethical
life as the impulse for justice and equity. These churches will see in
Matthew 9 a biblical warrant to deconstruct "sacrifice" as the immanent concern for "mercy." The benefit of this approach is a greater

4. Ibid., 245.
5. Ibid., 307.
6. Ibid., 308.
7. Ibid., 309.

capacity for inclusion and love. With the marginalization of disgust psychology, sociomoral boundaries are dismantled and hospitality is more easily extended.

Such are the positive benefits of moving the life of the church into the immanent frame. But Taylor's analysis also highlights the negative consequences of such a move. Specifically, with the collapse of the sacred, the immanent church will appear to function as a liberal, humanitarian, social-action group. No doubt many liberal Christians prefer this to the alternatives, a stigmatizing church that carves the world into "clean" and "unclean." But the immanent church may struggle with a sense of "flatness." The ritual life of the church, lacking a sacred dimension, may seem incongruous, vacuous, and irrelevant. In short, the entire existence and purpose of the church *as a church* is radically called into question.

I don't believe this analysis is anything particularly new. But we have, I think, approached some old issues from a novel direction. Specifically, although many worry about the toll liberalism is taking upon Christianity there has been one positive consequence in all this: the elimination of disgust psychology from the life of the church. And these benefits are considerable. The "liberal" church is less likely to mistake its cultic life for its mission in the world. That is, they will be less tempted by the Macbeth Effect. In a similar way, the "liberal" church will be more politically and socially engaged. Finally, the "liberal" church will be more open to otherness and difference.

Of course, I'm speaking in crude generalities. My only point is that a "liberal" movement—collapsing the sacred into the immanent —does go a fair way in eliminating the noxious effects of disgust psychology upon the life and mission of the church. The cost, however, is the loss of the transcendent, which calls the existence of the church *as a church* into question. Why be "religious" if liberal humanism is enough?

5.

Such is the path of elimination, the costs and benefits of removing disgust psychology from the life of the church. But is there another path? Might there be a way to retain the sacred dimension of faith while simultaneously controlling disgust psychology?

I want to conclude this book with a sketch of such a path. In contrast to the path of *elimination* this is a path of *regulation*. Common to both paths is the shared recognition that disgust psychology is inherently problematic and disruptive in the life of the church. We've documented these problems in great detail. So it seems clear that some prophylactic action in necessary. If disgust isn't *removed* from the faith community it needs vigilant *regulation*. How might this regulation be accomplished?

Recall the broad contours of the disgust domains, the various groupings of disgust stimuli:

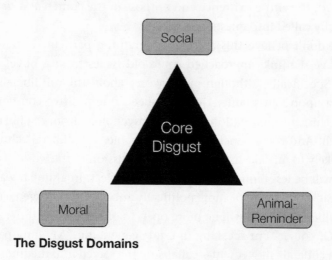

The Disgust Domains

At the center is *core disgust*, the adaptive nexus of the disgust response. All disgust responses build upon the innate psychology of core disgust. Thus, all disgust domains function as a boundary psychology. In core disgust the boundary is the physical body. Core disgust prevents the ingestion of harmful foodstuffs. In moral disgust, purity metaphors monitor moral "contaminants" that make a person "unclean." In social disgust, stigmatized groups are pushed out of the moral circle. And, finally, in animal-reminder disgust, the sacred and holy are separated from the animal and profane. Throughout this book we've pondered the dynamics in each domain, orienting our conversation around the issues of purity, hospitality, and mortality:

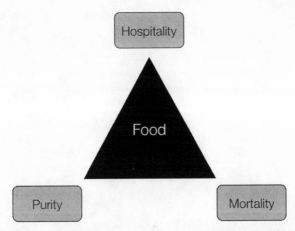

Core Disgust Regulating Purity, Hospitality, and Mortality

One way to summarize the problem of disgust is that when the moral domain is governed by a purity psychology, the pull becomes so overwhelming that the desire to be "clean," "pure," or "holy" begins to trump other considerations: the need, for example, to welcome others, or the importance of facing our own need and vulnerability. In short, as Miroslav Volf noted, the "will to purity" begins to dominate the faith experience. As we saw in our analyses of the events in Matthew 9 and 12, the pursuit of purity impairs the ability of the Pharisees to welcome others into table fellowship or to recognize their own need reflected in the needs of others.

We might call this dynamic "the purity collapse": the natural impulse to privilege purity over hospitality or a confrontation with human need. This is simply another way of explaining how disgust psychology tempts us to privilege the divinity dimension (holiness) over horizontal, human concerns. Sacrifice/purity begins to trump mercy.

When religious life comes to be dominated by holiness and purity categories, two things happen. First, social stigmas are created to protect our purity, pushing away people (e.g., "sinners") who are threats to our holiness. Second, the purity emphasis creates an otherworldly focus on the spiritual, eventually privileging the spiritual life over the life of the body. Religious life becomes "too spiritual" and begins to deny human need. This undermines empathy and justice:

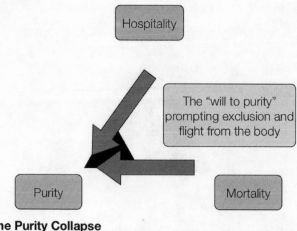

The Purity Collapse

Given these dynamics, how might we push against this "purity collapse"? How do we keep concerns over holiness and purity balanced with lives of mercy, hospitality, embrace, and a movement into the "fellowship of neediness"?

What is needed is a *regulating ritual* in the life of the church that pushes against the purity collapse, a ritual that keeps purity in tension with hospitality and an awareness of our biological vulnerability. For example, whenever hospitality is in danger of collapsing into a pursuit of purity this regulating ritual should keep the "will to embrace" firmly in view, functioning as a constant critique against the pursuit of isolation and quarantine. Further, whenever the pursuit of purity begins taking a Gnostic turn, bifurcating the physical and the spiritual, a ritual is required to remind us that the gritty and oozy realities of body cannot be left behind.

What ritual might serve these functions?

In the Introduction I made the observation that the dominant metaphors of the Eucharist precisely align with all four disgust domains: core, moral, social, and existential/mortal. The physical act of the Lord's Supper involves *food*, placing issues of core disgust at the center of the ritual. The act of oral incorporation activates the central psychological processes upon which all other aspects of disgust, problematically so, are built atop. That is, Christian understandings of purity, hospitality, and the relationship between the spirit and the body are regulated by the psychology of oral incorporation.

Built atop this ritual meal are the dominant metaphors of the Eucharist, each corresponding to a disgust domain. Purity psychology is activated in the Lord's Supper as the meal echoes the Day of Atonement, the ritual cleansing sacrifice of the Hebrews. As Christians participate in the Lord's Supper they remember that they are "washed in the blood of the Lamb" and made "white as snow." At the very same time, the Lord's Supper is a ritual enactment of Jesus' ministry of table fellowship. The Lord's Supper is a corporate ritual in which members practice welcome and hospitality. When we fail to "wait on each other," as we saw in the Corinthian church, something essential to the ritual has been lost and distorted. In short, the Lord's Supper activates the call to hospitality *along with an activation of purity metaphors*. By doing so, I am suggesting, the Eucharist functions as a regulating ritual. That is, the Eucharist helps keep purity psychology harnessed to and in tension with the call to hospitality. Embrace cannot be dislocated from purity. Consequently, it comes as no surprise that Paul, in his letter to the Corinthians, focuses his attention on the Eucharist to address the "divisions" among the Corinthian church. The Eucharist, properly practiced, regulates how the church experiences otherness and difference.

Finally, the Lord's Supper explicitly employs animal-reminder disgust stimuli. Believers drink the blood of Jesus and eat the body of Jesus. This cannibalistic metaphor was a shock in the first centuries of the church. It remains so. So why is this disgusting metaphor employed? Again, I think the issue is one of regulation. It is difficult to flee the body of Jesus and the implications of the Incarnation when the central ritual of Christian worship provides explicit reminders of the *body* and *blood* of Christ. What is interesting in all this, similar to the case with hospitality, is how the Eucharist is activating the psychology of purity *while simultaneously activating body-related disgust stimuli*. In the ritual, purity is tethered both to *hospitality* and to the *body*. This is important because if purity psychology is regularly activated the psychological effect will be (per the psychology discussed in this book) the gradual privileging of the spiritual over the physical, that the "brass tacks" of existence are slowly left behind in worship. But the Eucharist, as a regulating ritual, pushes against this Gnostic temptation by keeping the disgusting aspects of the body firmly in view. The Eucharist keeps Christian worship connected to the gritty, oozy realties of the human body.

In short, I believe that the Eucharist functions as a regulating ritual in the life of the church. I find it startling that the major metaphors of the Lord's Supper correspond, almost perfectly, with the disgust domains. However, I would be hesitant to say that the ritual and the meanings of the Lord's Supper were developed with the goal of using core disgust (food) to regulate the religious problems inherent in the other disgust domains. Regardless, I think it clear that the Eucharist can function as a disgust regulating ritual in the life of the church. The Lord's Supper holds each facet of disgust in tension, preventing the pull of the purity collapse. Consequently, the Lord's Supper allows the faith community to use purity metaphors while keeping those metaphors yoked with both hospitality and the body. This prevents the worst abuses of the purity collapse: stigmatizing otherness and fleeing from the implications of the Incarnation.

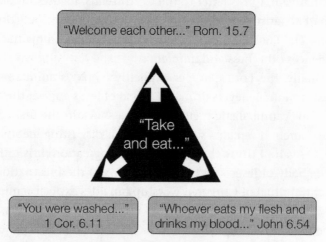

The Eucharist as a Regulative Ritual

Of course, recognizing the regulative function of the Eucharist doesn't imply that the ritual actually performs in this manner within a given faith community. But if this book has any recommendation it would be for churches to attend to and cultivate the tensions inherent in the celebration of the Eucharist. For it is in this ritual that holiness mixes with hospitality and an honest confrontation with our biological need and vulnerability. My suspicion is that a church which balances these tensions within the celebration of the Eucharist will be able to retain the experience of the holy and sacred while safely regulating the disgust psychology that naturally activates when appeals to purity or holiness are made. The Eucharist properly observed, I am suggesting, might allow the church to approach the sacred in a way that keeps the "will to embrace" from collapsing into the "will to purity." Disgust psychology is like a toxic acid. The Eucharist might allow the church to safely handle this hazardous material.

And yet, I am aware that this modest recommendation does not solve all the problems of disgust in the life of the church. Regardless, I think it remarkable that even when the purity collapse has occurred within a given faith community the metaphors of Eucharist are regularly activated, even if ignored. That is, even if a church is characterized by exclusion and hateful inhospitality the ritual of Eucharist regularly brings gospel stories, like the events in Matthew 9, back into the consciousness of the church. And one cannot help but wonder how the association of the Lord's Supper with Jesus' ministry of table fellowship might be shaping the missional imagination of that church. How, even if the adults were a lost cause, the image of Jesus eating with sinners might be affecting the minds of the children within that faith community. Or how the conscience of one individual might be pricked by the images of the Eucharist one Sunday morning, prompting her to reject the hurtful practices of the church. Deep in the Eucharist there exist these countervailing images that create unexpected tensions and associations. In the Eucharist, the swirling images of purity, hospitality, and body are continually refreshing the imagination of the church, week by week, generation by generation. Images that remind us, even when we are unaware, that God desires mercy, not sacrifice.

Bibliography

Ariès, Phillippe. *Western Attitudes toward Death: From the Middle Ages to the Present.* Baltimore: Johns Hopkins University Press, 1975.

Beck, Richard. "Feeling Queasy about the Incarnation: Terror Management Theory, Death, and the Body of Jesus." *Journal of Psychology and Theology* 36 (2008) 303–12.

———. "Profanity: The Gnostic Affront of the Seven Words You Can Never Say on Television." *Journal of Psychology and Theology* 37 (2009) 294–303.

Becker, Ernest. *The Birth and Death of Meaning: An Interdisciplinary Perspective on the Problem of Man.* 2nd ed. New York: Free Press, 1971.

———. *The Denial of Death.* New York: Simon & Schuster, 1973.

Belo, Fernando. *A Materialist Reading of the Gospel of Mark.* Maryknoll, NY: Orbis, 1981.

Bloom, Paul. *Descartes' Baby: How the Science of Child Development Explains What Makes Us Human.* New York: Basic, 2004.

Breznican, Anthony. "George Carlin responds to indecency uproar—with more than seven words." (March 13, 2004). Associated Press Archive, Record Number: D8196MO00.

Brown, Norman O. *Life Against Death: The Psychoanalytical Meaning of History.* Middletown, CT: Wesleyan University Press, 1959.

Brueggemann, Walter. *Theology of the Old Testament: Testimony, Dispute, Advocacy.* Minneapolis: Fortress, 1997.

Carrère, Sybil, and John M. Gottman. "Predicting Divorce Among Newlyweds from the First Three Minutes of a Marital Conflict Discussion." *Family Process* 38 (1999) 293–301.

Chapman, H. A., et al. "In Bad Taste: Evidence for the Oral Origins of Moral Disgust." *Science* 323 (2009) 1222–26.

Darwin, Charles. *The Expression of the Emotions in Man and Animals.* Chicago: University of Chicago Press, 1872/1965.

Demoulin, Stéphanie, et al. "Infrahumanization: The Differential Interpretation of Primary and Secondary Emotions." In *Intergroup Misunderstandings: Impact of Divergent Social Realities*, edited by Stéphanie Demoulin et al., 153–71. New York: Psychology, 2009.

Douglas, Mary. *Purity and Danger: An Analysis of the Concepts of Pollution and Taboo.* New York: Routledge, 1966.

Ekman, Paul, and W. V. Friesen. "Constants Across Cultures in the Face and Emotion." *Journal of Personality and Social Psychology* 17 (1971) 124–29.

Fallon, April E., et al. "The Child's Conception of Food: The Development of Food Rejections with Special Reference to Disgust and Contamination Sensitivity." *Child Development* 55 (1984) 566–75.

Gilmore, David. *Monsters: Evil Beings, Mythical Beasts, and All Manner of Imaginary Terrors*. Philadelphia: University of Pennsylvania Press, 2003.

Girard, Renè. *Things Hidden from the Foundation of the World*. Stanford, CA: Stanford University Press, 1987.

———. *Violence and the Sacred*. Baltimore: Johns Hopkins University Press, 1978.

Goldenberg, Jamie L., et al. "Death, Sex, Love, and Neuroticism: Why Is Sex Such a Problem?" *Journal of Personality and Social Psychology* 77 (1999) 1173–87.

———. "Fleeing the Body: A Terror Management Perspective on the Problem of Human Corporeality." *Personality and Social Psychology Review* 4 (2000) 200–218.

———. "I Am Not An Animal: Mortality Salience, Disgust, and the Denial of Human Creatureliness." *Journal of Experimental Psychology: General* 130 (2001) 427–35.

———. "Understanding Human Ambivalence about Sex: The Effects of Stripping Sex of Meaning." *Journal of Sex Research* 39 (2002) 310–20.

Gorer, Geoffrey. *Death, Grief, and Mourning*. Garden City, NY: Anchor, 1967.

Haidt, Jonathan, and Jesse Graham. "When Morality Opposes Justice: Conservatives Have Moral Intuitions That Liberals May Not Recognize." *Social Justice Research* 20 (2007) 98–116.

Haidt, Jonathan, and Sara Algoe. "Moral Amplification and the Emotions That Attach Us to Saints and Demons." In *Handbook of Experimental Existential Psychology*, edited by Jeff Greenberg et al., 322–35. New York: Guilford, 2004.

Haidt, Jonathan, et al. "Affect, Culture, and Morality, or Is It Wrong to Eat Your Dog?" *Journal of Personality and Social Psychology* 65 (1993) 613–28.

———. "Individual Differences in Sensitivity to Disgust: A Scale Sampling Seven Domains of Disgust Elicitors." *Personality and Individual Differences* 16 (1994) 701–13.

Heath, Chip, et al. "Emotional Selection in Memes: The Case of Urban Legends." *Journal of Personality and Social Psychology* 81 (2001) 1028–41.

Heim, S. Mark. *Saved from Sacrifice: A Theology of the Cross*. Grand Rapids: Eerdmans, 2006.

Lakoff, George, and Mark Johnson. *Metaphors We Live By*. Chicago: University of Chicago Press, 1980.

Lakoff, George, and Mark Johnson. *Philosophy in the Flesh: The Embodied Mind and Its Challenge to Western Thought*. New York: Basic, 1999.

Lee, Philip. *Against the Protestant Gnostics*. New York: Oxford University Press, 1987.

Levi-Strauss, Claude. *Race and History*. Paris: UNESCO, 1952.

Leyens, Jacques-Philippe, et al. "Psychological Essentialism and the Differential Attribution of Uniquely Human Emotions to Ingroups and Outgroups." *EJSP* 31 (2001) 395–411.

McGill, Arthur C. *Life and Death: An American Theology*. Eugene, OR: Wipf & Stock, 1987.

———. *Suffering: A Test of Theological Method*. Eugene, OR: Wipf & Stock. 1982.

Miller, William Ian. *The Anatomy of Disgust*. Cambridge: Harvard University Press, 1997.

Nemeroff, Carol, and Paul Rozin. "The Makings of the Magical Mind." In *Imagining the Impossible: Magical, Scientific, and Religious Thinking in Children*, 1–34. New York: Cambridge University Press, 2000.

Nussbaum, Martha. *Hiding from Humanity: Disgust, Shame, and the Law*. Princeton, NJ: Princeton University Press, 2004.

Pinker, Steven. *The Blank Slate: The Modern Denial of Human Nature*. New York: Penguin, 2002.

Pinker, Steven. *The Stuff of Thought: Language as a Window into Human Nature*. New York: Viking, 2007.

Pohl, Christine D. *Making Room: Recovering Hospitality as a Christian Tradition*. Grand Rapids: Eerdmans, 1999.

Rollins, Peter. *The Orthodox Heretic: And Other Impossible Tales*. Brewster, MA: Paraclete, 2009.

Rozin, Paul, and April E. Fallon. "A Perspective on Disgust." *Psychological Review* 94 (1987) 23–41.

Rozin, Paul, et al. "Disgust." In *Handbook of Emotions*, 2nd ed., edited by Michael Lewis et al., 637–53. New York: Guilford, 2000.

———. "Operation of the Laws of Sympathetic Magic in Disgust and Other Domains." *Journal of Personality and Social Psychology* 50 (1986) 703–12.

———. "Sensitivity to Indirect Contacts With Other Persons: AIDS Aversion as a Composite of Aversion to Strangers, Infection, Moral Taint, and Misfortune." *Journal of Applies Psychology* 103 (1994) 495–505.

———. "The CAD Hypothesis: A Mapping Between Three Moral Emotions (Contempt, Anger, Disgust) and Three Moral Codes (Community, Autonomy, Divinity)." *Journal of Personality and Social Psychology* 76 (1999) 574–86.

Shweder, Robert, et al. "The 'Big Three' of Morality (Autonomy, Community, Divinity) and the 'Big Three' Explanations of Suffering." In *Morality and Health*, edited by Allan M. Brandt and Paul Rozin, 119–69. New York: Routledge, 1997.

Singer, Peter. *The Expanding Circle: Ethics and Sociobiology*. New York: Farrar, Straus & Giroux, 1981.

Taylor, Charles. *A Secular Age*. Cambridge, MA: Belknap, 2007.

Volf, Miroslav. *Exclusion and Embrace: A Theological Exploration of Identity, Otherness, and Reconciliation*. Nashville, TN: Abington, 1996.

Wallace, David Foster. *This is Water*. New York: Little Brown, 2009.

Wells, Samuel. *Improvisation: The Drama of Christian Ethics*. Grand Rapids: Brazos, 2004.

Williamson, Beth. *Christian Art: A Very Short Introduction*. Oxford: Oxford University Press, 2004

Witherington, Ben. *Conflict and Community in Corinth*. Grand Rapids: Eerdmans, 1995.

Zhong, Chen-Bo, and Katie Liljenquist. "Washing Away Your Sins: Threatened Morality and Physical Cleansing." *Science* 313 (2006) 1451–52.